Those Naughty Ladies
of the Old Northwest

by
Gary and Gloria Meier

— A Maverick Publication —

Maverick Publications
Drawer 5007 • Bend, Oregon 97708

DEDICATION

To JWA, who planted the seed.

FRONTISPIECE

The world loves a spice of wickedness.
—Longfellow

Table of Contents

FOREWORD

This is a book about the world's oldest profession as practiced in the hectic, free-swinging days of the Pacific Northwest. It is a collection of stories, anecdotes, and legends about the colorful madams and the girls and the parlor houses in Oregon and Washington from the mid-1800s to the first decade of this century.

This is not a book of judgment. For despite the antiquity of the business, prostitution has a sort of historical ambiguity. Societies from the time of the Sumerians (circa 4,000 B.C.), who recorded the first reference to prostitution, to the present have never been able to decide if prostitution is good or evil, natural or deviant, a crime, a sin, or a necessary service.

There is no doubt that many northwestern men had sentimental and tender feelings for the women who helped them endure the hard life in the woods, on the ranches, and in the mines. Ladies such as French Rita, Carrie Belle, Oregon Rose, and Madam Lou Graham were remembered affectionately by men in the Northwest timber and gold country. No matter how isolated and unreachable a mining or logging settlement was, the nymphs of the night mysteriously appeared just as the last nail was driven in the saloons.

The complete story of the brothels of the Old West has never been properly written, and perhaps never can be, since no one kept notes and the people who lived them are no longer here to tell us. Besides, most of the sisterhood traveled frequently and lightly, preferring to leave their pasts and identities behind. The business of the ladies of joy was pleasing customers, not obliging future historians.

However, enough anecdotes, letters, diaries, and newspaper accounts exist to give us a sort of keyhole glimpse into the lives of the ladies of ill repute. The stories and photographs are the result of three years of research, and are representative of the red-light business throughout the West in those rowdy early years.

One further point should be made before turning the reader over to The Ladies. Most books about prostitution are written from the sociological perspective. Certainly disease, misery, and violence were companions to many of the girls as they plied their ancient trade in the Northwest. But this book is not intended as a study of the dark aspects of the business. This is a collection of tales from the rollicking, often humorous, lighter side of the game. These stories have been pulled from the hidden, musty pages of forgotten journals, court records, and newspapers and present an entertaining look at a small part of the Northwest's colorful past.

Those who believe that history must be solemn, boring, and humorless to have merit will not like this book.

For the others, here are *Those Naughty Ladies of the Old Northwest.*

Gary & Gloria Meier
Eugene, Oregon
November 1988

CHAPTER ONE
The Business

One of the Pacific Northwest's earliest classes of entrepreneurs was that collection of shady ladies known as "sporting girls," "daughters of joy," "painted ladies," and "girls of the line." Although the chief motivation of these fair businesswomen was to lighten the burden of men's pockets, they were welcomed, sought after, and cherished by a large segment of the lonely male population in the early Northwest.

As elsewhere in the West, the ladies of ultimate accessibility came to Oregon and Washington as soon as settlements were started and on the heels of every gold strike. Most moved on, but some stayed to reach high in their calling by establishing wondrous and notorious first-class parlor houses where only genteel, wealthy gentlemen were welcomed as guests. Madam Fanshaw's Mansion of Sin in Portland, Josey Tripp's fine house in Spokane, and Lou Graham's place in Seattle were widely known along the Pacific Coast as elite pleasure palaces where graciousness and decorum were maintained. There were many others.

The usual working locale for the ladies was a rollicking wide-open section of town known as the "red-light district." The term "red-light district" originated in Dodge City, Kansas, from a custom among uninhibited railroaders of leaving their red brakeman's lanterns hanging outside the door of their girl of the evening to discourage intruders. In small mining and logging camps the district was also known as "the line" and "the row." In the cities it was the "tenderloin," coined for an area in New York City where vice reigned.

In Portland, the district was known as the North End and Whitechapel, after the famous sin area of London. Seattle's

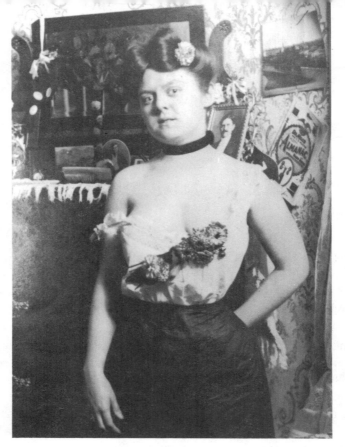

This sporting girl chose to follow the red-light path in the Northwest.

girls were mostly located south of Yesler Way in an area known as the Lava Bed and "Down on the Sawdust" (for the old mill refuse there). Spokane's tenderloin ranged along Main and Front (now Trent) Avenues, from Mill (now Wall) Street to Market on the east. Tacoma's red lights were chiefly found on upper Pacific Avenue, "Opera Alley," and in the "D" Street area. Olympia had its Lower Town, south of Third Street, and in rowdy Aberdeen there was Huron Street and "Paradise Alley."

The profession in which the ladies sought to make their fortunes was divided into four categories: parlor houses, brothels, boxhouses, and the line.

The old-time parlor house was at the top of the scale for *filles de joie*. Most parlor houses were elegant, some were downright palatial and all were more sumptuous than the other categories of bordellos. They boasted luxurious furnishings, running to red velvet, gold, and white lace, and many of them provided music and fine liquors. They exuded grace and charm, and the ladies who worked in the best parlor houses were the prettiest and most accomplished in the business. And they made the most money.

A visit to a well-run parlor house was much like a visit to an upper crust private home, and the girls residing there resembled in beauty, refinement, and dress, the daughters of the house. Indeed there were claims that the only difference was that the "doves" were more attractive, more intelligent, and more cultured than the young society ladies.

True parlor houses were usually found in the larger towns and cities of the Northwest, but there were exceptions in some of the richer small mining towns. Julie Bowdrie's house in lively, gold-rich Jacksonville, in southern Oregon, was success-ful for many years in a town of a couple of thousand people, most of them lonely miners. And in the silver mining camp of Ruby City, Washington Territory, Madam Jennie Bright's

Much of Spokane's red-light business was centered around Main Avenue in the early 1900s.

The entire upper floor of this building on Tacoma's Pacific Avenue was given over to local "businesswomen" to ply their time-honored trade. Circa 1892.

One of Rae McRoberts' two elegant Seattle parlor houses.

Some claimed that the girls in a high-class parlor house were more attractive, more intelligent, and more cultured than many young society ladies. Pictured here is Annie Williams of Madam Lou Graham's famous Seattle establishment.

elegant establishment catered to a population of only four- or five-hundred.

Visitors to a parlor house, almost always the wealthy and influential gentlemen of the city, would be shown to an ornate roomy parlor by the madam or a maid. If the customer was not calling on a specific girl, one was either chosen by the madam and sent to join him or he was allowed to select for himself. The chosen lady then provided a time of relaxed, witty, intelligent conversation amid plush and opulent surroundings during which the guest was offered a fine wine or champagne. One of the talented residents might play the piano or violin, and often there were games of chance for the amusement of the visitor.

In the top parlor houses everything was conducted with the utmost propriety and dignity while any hint of commercialism was kept to a minimum. When the gentleman was eventually ready to be taken upstairs by his lady, it was the madam who politely brought up the matter of fees in order to maintain the social distinction between a parlor house and commercial brothel where the girl had to collect her own fee. The guest would then be escorted to an elegantly furnished bedroom to enjoy the primary purpose of his visit.

The parlor house was not often found in a well-known red-light district because to locate there would have gone against the image of tasteful "respectability."

Madam Julie Bowdrie of Jacksonville poses pensively
for the photographer.

This is a view of girls and clients relaxing with a game of cards in a parlor house.

Lila Young's parlor house, Seattle, Washington.

Brothels were far more numerous than parlor houses and consisted chiefly of hotels, rooming houses, and small apartments over saloons. Some brothels were nearly as elegant as the parlor houses, the main differences being lower fees and a madam with less exacting requirements for the girls' appearance and decorum.

The greatest majority of brothels appeared to be simple boarding houses or hotels, but in reality they did little to solicit overnight guests. They frequently located in recognized red-light districts, and in many small communities one rooming

Many Northwest brothels appeared to be simple hotels or rooming houses, but they did little to encourage a legitimate trade.

house was the entire red-light district. For example, in the tiny Willamette River wheat-shipping port of Butteville, Oregon, Miss Enna Camouline and two female "cousins" kept a "rooming house" for a number of years on Union Street, in the shadow of the large Episcopal church which dominated the town. Their's was the only house for many miles in an area of staunch, no-nonsense, religious settlers. They catered primarily to the riverboat crews, and an occasional farmer's son out for a furtive fling.

In the open Wild West town of Pendleton, Oregon, there were seventeen brothels in the early 1800s, most of which masqueraded as ordinary hotels. The Oak Hotel, the Columbia Hotel, the St. George, and the Oregon Hotel, among others, had a continuous supply of ladies who provided comfort to cowhands, sheepherders, and railroaders. Some of the buildings stand to this day. In the now empty Oregon Hotel there was once the notorious "Chapel Room" where customers waited in former church pews facing a minister's lectern to meet the girls.

Brothels came in all shapes and sizes, depending on the market. Some were little row houses such as those found in Portland's North End in the 1880s and 1890s. Small one-and-a-half and two-story wooden buildings lined the streets north of Burnside like little shops, each with a window facing the street and a girl seated inside. Some of the dwellings were gorgeously furnished and the halls paneled with beautifully grained expensive wood. Over many of the front doors was a girl's name—Liz, Georgia, Jennie, May, The Favorite, and others.

Some brothels were immense. Seattle's flamboyant mayor Hiram Gill had one built overlooking the waterfront with five-hundred rooms—the largest bordello in the world. (See story in Chapter 5.)

Port Townsend's brothels were located along the waterfront on Water Street. There was a saying for many years that "sin flourishes at sea level." The Good Women and the rest of polite society lived, shopped, and stayed high on the bluff overlooking the lower town.

The spirited brothels of wild Aberdeen, on Washington's Grays Harbor were located right along the main street for years. This small but lively seaport was known up and down

The large Episcopal church of Butteville, Oregon (top center) cast a stern shadow over Miss Enna Camouline's "rooming house." (Not shown.)

Aberdeen, Washington, was a wild, open seaport with a large concentration of bawdy belles and bordellos. Its sin district was known by sailors the world over.

The old-time western saloon was a common link between lonely miners, loggers, and cowhands and the sporting girls.

This 1890s rural pleasure house, operated by May Graves, was located on the Columbia River near Portland.

This is the main house at the rural ranch bordello of William and Ella Stiles, near Sumpter, Oregon.

the coast for its free and easy "sporting" life. Loggers and sailors flocked to Aberdeen's notorious Huron Street where they joyfully did what they could to assure the financial success of the "nymphs of the night."

Many of the brothels in Aberdeen—and there were many—were located over saloons. The Diamond Front, the Merry Widow, the Klondike, the Lion, and the My House saloons, and many others, were well-known for their ladies of pleasure. Nell Blanton, buxom proprietress of the Pioneer Saloon and Rooms, did such a popular business that she was able to carry out the plan of many of her sisters—she retired and raised horses in Southern California.

The old-time western saloon was a common link between lonely miners, loggers, and cowhands and the sporting girls. Some saloons were "respectable," of course, but many catered tacitly, and often enthusiastically, to customers' thirsts for other than liquor. Occasionally a madam or ambitious working girl would see the opportunities in combining a house and saloon, as did Nell Blanton. In the historic Columbia River trading center of The Dalles, there were two successful house-saloon combines operated by women. Irish Moll's Place and Madam DeBilk's Golden Rule were known along the Columbia and into the ranching and gold country as the places to visit in The Dalles to slake two kinds of thirst.

Another type of brothel found in the Pacific Northwest was the rural house, operating for soldiers near an outpost or as a service along freight routes. These bordellos, incorporated into a ranching operation, usually functioned under the management of a husband-wife team. They generally were not large ventures, most having from three to six girls. One such enterprise was the ranch of William and Ella Stiles in the rich gold country of the Sumpter Valley in northeastern Oregon. "Ma" Stiles, a former madam from Kentucky, employed several girls to give comfort to passing miners and freighters going to

Madam Ella Stiles was called "Ma" by her girls.

This photo shows the interior of an 1890s boxhouse in Spokane,
Washington. The "pretty waiter girls" would accommodate customers with
more than liquor in the curtained booths at the upper left and right
of the photograph.

and from Sumpter, Granite, and Auburn. The continuing flow
of doves who resided at the Stiles ranch had a life free from
many of the normal hazards in the rowdy mining camps. In
their off hours they could be seen roaming the ranch grounds
on Stiles' horses, and on holidays such as the Fourth of July,
"Ma" and her husband would take the girls into Sumpter by
wagon to attend the parade and picnic.

Some of the most popular brothels in larger towns and cities
were the type known as "variety theaters," or "boxhouses."
The variety theater was a combination of burlesque theater,
saloon, dance hall, and bordello. They were places of
abandoned gaiety which played to the desires of work-weary
loggers and heavy-pocketed miners in from the hills.

The typical boxhouse consisted of a concert hall with a stage
at one end and a bar at the other. The main floor had tables for
drinking, card playing, watching the lewd and vaudeville-type
shows, and getting to know the waitresses. The chief feature of

the boxhouse was one or two mezzanine tiers or curtained cubicles which gave the places their name. In the cubicles the real performances went on in most of the variety theaters.

The boxhouses employed ladies known and advertised as "pretty waiter girls." They wore gaudy costumes designed to display and accentuate their charms. The chief purpose of the pretty waiter girls was to entice customers into buying liquor. Lots of liquor. For the boxhouse variety theaters did not make their profits from admissions, which usually started at ten cents, but from the liquor sold to patrons as they watched the show, and from the gambling tables. The costumed lovelies spent some time conversing with customers, plying them with drinks and teases, and often would lead them to an upstairs cubicle for other, more expensive, performances.

Boxhouse owner Tom Dwyer of Portland clad his pretty waiter girls in short red jackets, black stockings, fancy garters, red slippers—and nothing else! Attendance increased enormously at his place until law officers modified his dress code.

The stage show performers included singers, dancers, and traveling "actresses" who would put on bawdy skits to gleeful howls from the audience. But the more frequent stage entertainment came from the pretty waiter girls who would go up on the stage to perform a spicy dance or to sing with a voice resembling a frightened mountain goat.

The undisputed king of the boxhouses was a wily Seattle showman named John Considine. In 1891, after managing a lucrative variety theater in the red-light district for a year, he bought the business outright. His People's Theater remained profitable, even through the blight of the 1893 depression that ruined much of Seattle's economy.

But in 1894 the good city fathers, in a short-lived attempt at cleaning up the sin area known as "south of Yesler," passed an ordinance prohibiting the sale of liquor in theaters. This was a distressful blow to John, who decided to switch his base of operations to a more reasonable city, such as Spokane.

He owned a similar enterprise, also called the People's Theater, in Spokane for three years, but his business became more controversial than profitable and he returned to Seattle in 1897. By now the silliness of the reform movement was over

As "pretty waiter girls" attend customers on the main floor, a traveling "aotress" performs on stage in a boxhouse. Many of the female stage performers were available after the show in the upper-floor cubicles.

and Considine reopened his original People's Theater at Second and Washington. Business was better than ever, and soon he owned several other boxhouses scattered throughout Seattle's Tenderloin.

One of John Considine's stage performers at the People's Theater was a vivacious, charming, redheaded dancer named Kitty Rockwell, who was soon to become famous in the Yukon as "Klondike Kate."

Kitty was a Northwest girl. Though born in Kansas in 1876, she was raised in Spokane Falls by her mother and step-father. The young redhead was a lively, impetuous girl, whose strong will was difficult to control. She was sent away to different boarding schools, but that did not help as she was expelled for her saucy, outlandish behavior, such as dancing and carrying on with men. At one school, a convent, Kitty managed to collect seven diamond rings, which she had to return when found out by the horrified Sisters.

Klondike Kate, the Queen of the Yukon, was also a
Pacific Northwest girl.

Home again in Spokane Falls, Kitty was far from being a proper young lady by 1890 standards. Because she lived only for fun and parties, flirting with each "Dapper Dan" that came her way, her mother decided to take the girl on a sea voyage to New York for a change of scene and some strict supervision. Things did not work out the way mother planned, though, because in New York her daughter, under the name "Kitty Phillips," got a job as a chorus girl in a variety theater. One job followed another in the variety halls of Manhattan and in the fast action and bright lights of Coney Island, but Kitty yearned for the West.

Returning once again to her home town, Spokane, Kitty completed her "finishing-school" in the boxhouses of the boisterous lumber town. While she preferred being an on-stage performer, working the floor was more profitable. The now seasoned boxhouse girl wandered for a time throughout the Northwest following new opportunities.

Finally, she worked her way to Seattle, the big, noisy, brawling, utterly wicked sin capital of the Pacific Northwest. Kitty Rockwell and Seattle took to each other immediately, and soon she was working for Big John Considine in his infamous People's Theater.

Kitty did not stay long in Seattle, however, because yet another, grander adventure was beckoning her. Gold had been discovered in the Yukon, causing the biggest gold rush in history, and Kitty wanted to be right in the middle of it. If there was one thing the lusty redhead had learned in the rough towns of the Northwest, it was that a girl could do quite well by mining the miners. So she went to Dawson to pan the boys' pokes and win their hearts. She was pretty and ambitious and soon the sourdoughs dubbed her "Klondike Kate, the Queen of the Yukon."

She rode high on the gold rush, sporting $300 hats and $1,000 gowns. But also during this time she began an intense relationship that was to end as one of the great tragedies in her life. She took up with a cagey Greek boxhouse waiter named Alexander Pantages. She grubstaked him for five years while he rose from waiter to wealthy theatrical magnate, but in the end he jilted Kate and married a girl from "the right side of the tracks." Kate claimed he had promised to marry her and she sued him. She was to receive only a token settlement.

After the Yukon days lost their spark for Kate, she worked in various variety theaters and dance halls throughout the Northwest. In 1914 she settled on a desert claim in the sagebrush plains east of Bend, Oregon. The Queen of the Yukon was thirty-nine years old. In the mid-twenties she moved to a rustic home on Franklin Street in Bend, where she lived for many years. Kate was a controversial figure in Bend, "Aunt Kate" to some, "our destitute prostitute" to others. She worked at whatever cooking and cleaning jobs she could find to get by, her wealth from the Far North having long since

The Theater Comique was the infamous Tacoma
boxhouse of Harry Morgan, king of the vice district.

escaped her.

In 1933 Kate entered into a strange marriage to an old sourdough named Johnny Matson. After the ceremony, he returned to his Yukon claim and Kate stayed in Bend. They wrote letters and got together yearly in the spring, though Johnny never came to Bend. He died in the North in 1946.

At the age of seventy-one, two years after Matson's death, Kate married again, this time to a longtime friend, Bill Van Duren. They settled in the Willamette Valley town of Sweet Home, where Klondike Kate Rockwell, of Spokane, Seattle, and the Yukon, died in 1957 at eighty years of age.

John Considine also had great success with a pretty waiter girl named Louise Gething. Louise, formerly employed in a Spokane parlor house, was a pretty, petite, slim, redhead who provided John with a gimmick that proved highly profitable to both of them. She would mount the stage, appearing nervous. She would then begin to sing the one song she knew. It was a ballad which began: "The boat lies high, the boat lies low; she lies high and dry on the Ohio." This she sang in a quavering falsetto, invariably bursting into tears at the last note. She so

This 1899 photograph of "the line" in Dawson during the Klondike gold rush is an example of the red-light row houses in mining and logging towns throughout the Pacific Northwest.

Unidentified girl of the line in eastern Washington.

obviously required protection against the cruel blasts of the
world that many gentlemen chivalrously responded. She then
selected and took upstairs the one who appeared to be the
wealthiest.

The high-spirited Gay '90s boxhouse of Big Bill McGowan in
Olympia, Tom Dwyer in Portland, Considine of Seattle, and
Harry Morgan's Theater Comique in Tacoma, and the lively
Olympus in Aberdeen, were subjects of nostalgic memories far

into this century for many elderly northwestern gentlemen.

The final category of working places inhabited by the bawdy belles was "the line." In almost all of the logging, gold mining, and railroad construction camps there was a certain section on the edge of town reserved for the girls of the line. These were usually short rows of small shanties, also called cribs, which housed those soiled doves that could not or wished not to gain employment in a larger bordello or parlor house.

The girls of the line were close to the action and the popular ones often had their own line waiting outside their door. Some of the more delightfully raucous sounding names in the history of American sporting girls comes from placards which hung over the doors of gold camp girls. Such intriguing appellations as: The Oregon Mare; Light Handle Liz; The Dancing Fawn; Lucy Give 'Em Back; and Billy Goat Belle were attached to ladies of the line in Washington and Oregon mining settlements of Alamo, Gimletville, Desolation, Ruby City, Cracker City, and Bonanza.

A closer look at the ladies of the red-lights should properly begin with those rulers in velvet gloves, the "top-sergeants" of the trade—The Madams.

CHAPTER TWO
The Madams

John Steinbeck wrote this about madams: "Every town has its celebrated madams, eternal women to be sentimentalized down the years. There is something very attractive to men about a madam. She combines the brains of a businessman, the toughness of a prize fighter, the warmth of a companion, the humor of a tragedian."

There were all kinds of madams. The good ones ran quiet, stately, decent, clean, honest, sporting houses where a man could take his ease in safety and comfort. The madam played many roles to guests and girls. She was counselor, medical authority, philosopher, keeper of secrets, and giver of private loans. She was often a philanthropist, contributing heavily to every charity.

The madam who was truly called to her profession was the essence of motherness. She schooled her girls in grace and charm. She saw to their needs, served them when they were sick, listened to their troubles, and answered them in matters of love.

The girls in a well-run house were very like the madam, partly because she hired that kind and partly because a good madam imprinted herself on the house. A guest could stay a very long time in a house run by a skilled madam before hearing an ugly word or being subjected to any unpleasantness or discomfort.

The job of madamship was not easy. She took care of all financial transactions, which required, in a large house, considerable bookkeeping skills. She had to deal with dressmakers to make certain her girls were stylish and well-dressed. She had to bargain with food and liquor merchants to ensure

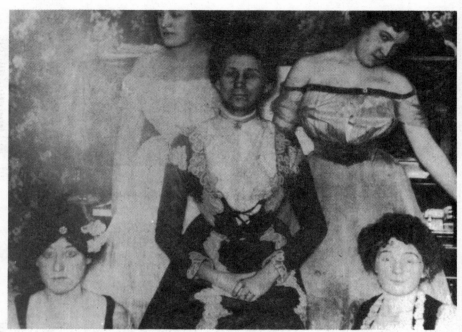

An unidentified Tacoma madam and her sporting ladies.

The lady in this circa 1910 photograph, from the
Seattle Police Department archives, is identified only
as "a madam of the Restricted District."

These Northwest sporting house nymphs pose for a portrait.

that her standards of excellence were met. And she had to always, *always* be concerned with "the boys downtown"—the law officers and courts and other powers who felt they had to extract a tribute. Most madams paid a monthly fine for operating a disorderly house, which amounted to a "license" to operate.

The professional madam who aspired to a long, profitable career was honest in her dealings with customers and their money. Wealthy men often left large sums in her safe with no fear that it would disappear.

According to a story told in northeastern Oregon, one night a La Grande businessman, who happened to be a favorite guest of Madam Julie Harbor, came to see her and asked if they could speak privately. She took him to a room and he confided to her that he had a lot of money on him which some men intended to take away. He wanted to leave it in her care until the next day when he could get it to a bank.

Then he pulled out a leather pouch containing more money than Julie had ever seen before. He said there was $50,000 in the bundle. He gave her the pouch and left.

Julie kept the money in her safe and told no one. For two days she waited for him to return, but he did not show up. She was frightened at having all that money in her care and became suspicious of each new guest.

After a week, she learned that the man who gave her the money had been injured and was in a Baker City hotel, sixty miles to the south by rail. Julie went to Baker City and found her man in bed unconscious. He had been beaten and battered almost beyond recognition. The doctors had filled him with morphine and it took Julie over an hour to rouse him. He could not recall what had happened to him, but thought the thugs had taken his money. When Julie informed him that the money—all of it—was safely locked away at her house he was incredulous and grateful.

Julie's businessman friend soon recovered and returned to La Grande to get his money. When he left Julie's place, however, he was short $2,000. That was the amount he gave her for her honesty.

Madam Julie Harbor, of La Grande, Oregon, is shown here (third from right), along with some of her girls.

The successful madam seldom worked as a prostitute herself because to do so would have placed her in competition with her girls, possibly causing dissent among them. The madam was the executive of the house and confined her activities to its management. But there were exceptions.

Vena Blanchard ran a dignified, proper parlor house in Yakima. The Northern Pacific railroad had moved the entire town, building by building, north ten miles from the old site of Yakima City the year before in 1885. The new town was booming when Vena established her house and she was an immediate success.

Vena was beautiful with her long brown hair, ready smile, delicate features, and laughing eyes. Her evening wear ran to lovely brown satin gowns, trimmed with white lace. During the cold Yakima Valley winters, Vena wore stylish fur hats and a long brown marten coat. Never the one to appear a bordello girl, Vena preferred her outfits with high necks. At her throat she always wore a single emerald on a gold chain that had been given to her by a former employer in Creede, Colorado, one Jefferson Randolph Smith—"Soapy" Smith.

Since her early days as a dove in one of Soapy's brothels in Creede, before the gambler and con man went north to Skagway to get killed, Vena loved men and she loved her work. In Yakima, still in her 30s and now a real madam with her own place, Vena could see no reason to love men less. So she loved them more. She worked right alongside her girls, so to speak, and if it was cause for dissension in the house no record remains. Vena's activities caused no trouble because she was a high draw and ran a very popular, profitable establishment, and that profited the girls, also.

Vena Blanchard was the darling of local railroad officials and Yakima business leaders. She was often seen on the arm of one well-known gentleman or another, entering Switzer's Opera House on Front Street, or at a well-attended soiree in town.

Thus, while some madams "did not," Vena "did." Although, as a former patron said of her, "When you sat down in the parlor and started talking to Vena, you often forgot what it was you came for."

Living conditions in a house run by a good madam,

particularly a parlor house, were pleasant for the girls. They were coddled, protected, well-fed, and well-dressed. It was a common procedure for the girls to purchase fine clothes and other accessories from the best stores and dressmakers on the madams' accounts.

Meal accommodations were arranged to fit the schedules of the house. In Rae McRoberts' fine parlor house in Seattle, breakfast for the girls was served promptly at 2:00 o'clock in the afternoon, with the choice of eggs, clam cakes with bacon, kidney saute, shad roe, breast of chicken, buttered toast, and coffee or milk. Rae always came downstairs for breakfast, but the girls had the choice of sitting at the table or having breakfast served in their rooms.

Dinner, the principal meal of the day, was served at six o'clock, which allowed time for primping before the nightly performance. The ladies enjoyed having guests at mealtimes. They often lingered over dinner until after eight o'clock, and

Rae McRoberts, popular and well-known Seattle
parlor house madam.

Two Seattle parlor house ladies wait by the ever-present piano.

then rose only when needed in the front rooms. A light supper was available around midnight.

Music was frequently part of the life at a house run by a good madam. Pianos were commonly seen in the nicer houses of ill repute. Madam Lou Graham, Seattle's famous parlor house operator, had a gold piano for years. Annie Baylor of Coos Bay (then called Marshfield), Oregon, was accomplished on the violin. Often one of the girls in a house could play an instrument, and did.

There was another way that music was brought into a house. Many early variety or vaudeville musicians used to tarry for a week or so in the towns and cities of the Northwest. Sometimes a madam and her girls would attend a matinee performance of the stage bill and if they took a fancy to a pianist, or any other instrumentalist, they would invite him to live at their house during his stay in town. This kindness was returned by free musical performances at the house for the girls and guests.

Not only the care, but the training of young "boarders" was an integral part of madamship. Not all the ladies aspiring to the better money and conditions in a nicer brothel or parlor house had the charm, grace, or decorum needed for success by a *fille de joie* in a fine establishment. It was solely up to the madam to instill those qualities.

If a former girl of the line or a fresh recruit new to the

Annie Baylor of Marshfield often played her violin for
the entertainment of clients.

Jessie Clark, pictured here in 1898, was one of Seattle's madam Lila Young's top draws. The parlor house girls were the prettiest and most accomplished in the business.

This is the only known photograph of Madam Eve Johnson of Spokane.

business had the right potential—attractiveness and ambition—the madam took charge of the young lady's schooling to correct whatever deficiencies might be present. Manners, courtesy, conversational ability, patience, and pleasing personality traits had to become natural to the girl. She had to learn propriety and respect for each client's reputation. She had to know that a proper, professional dove never spoke to a man on the street, although he may have been with her in the house the night before. She learned the right way to visit a patron who was too sick or too wealthy to come to the house. It was the madam's job to teach.

How a working girl came to be a madam is a study in early entrepreneurship. No lady inexperienced in the business could simply buy a house, hire some girls, and decide she was a madam. It did not work that way; there were too many subtleties to the profession, too much to know. An apprenticeship had to be served.

The madams of the Northwest first put in their time as girls of the house elsewhere. Some had served as doves in Washington and Oregon, but due to the transient nature of the business most came from other areas of the country. Spokane

This was how the well-run house of Olympia's madam Billie Witham
appeared in 1899. The two men on either side of Madam Billie may be
customers or employees.

This is a view of Spokane's Front Avenue (now Trent Avenue) as Madam
Eve Johnson saw it in the late 1870s.

Retired Madam Belle Bernard of Seattle.

madam Eve Johnson had worked at New York's famed Seven Sisters; Billie Witham of Olympia came from Madam Bertha Kahn's establishment in San Francisco; Portland's Miss Minnie Holmes and two of her girls put in time with Kate Townsend in New Orleans; and Belle Bernard of Seattle came out of the world-famous Everleigh Club in Chicago.

If a bright, ambitious working girl had the spark and confidence for business, and was willing to risk an often lucrative job working for someone else, she could open a place of her own—if she had the money or connections—and become a Madam of the Trade.

Advertising was an important business tool for the madams. Much of the advertising was done in the time-honored tradition of "word of mouth" by happy customers. In addition, many

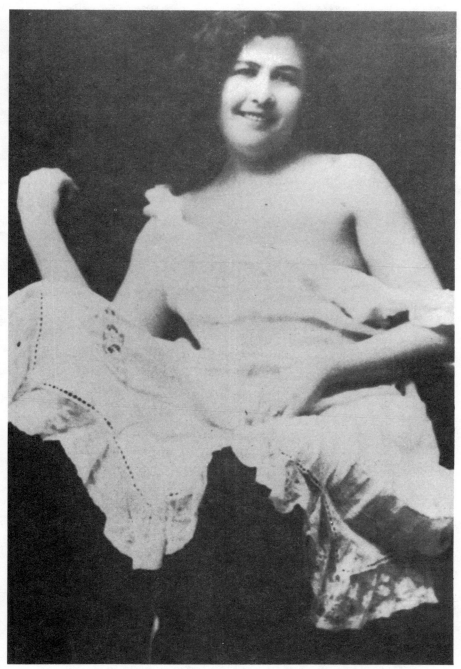

This "publicity still" of an unidentified red-light girl is an example of a
common means of advertising in the old days.

madams hired male and female steering people, called "cappers," to work in the saloons where they would tout the advantages of this or that brothel. Some madams and girls in the Northwest had business cards printed with their names and often a flowery message of love or an imprint of a symbol such as a red heart.

Another common method of advertising, popular among clients, was the "soiree" (SWA-RAY). The madams would send out engraved invitations to the most prominent men in the city. The reception was very correct, nothing rude, everything refined and elegant. It was astonishing to see the class of

The parlor house soiree was a festive meeting of sin
and society.

gentlemen who gathered at a parlor house soiree; business and city leaders, legislators, lobbyists, judges (in certain cities at certain times), celebrities of the day—all of what was considered the upper class of society.

At the soiree the best suppers were served and the finest wines and liquors provided. The entire evening often cost the madam a thousand dollars or more, but she was always able to recoup the expense from the guests who chose to stay the night. The soiree was a convenient fun way to advertise the house and a good method of enticing new clients and introducing established clients to a new girl.

But the most flamboyant way of advertising, which also showed the tolerance which held forth in cities of the Northwest in earlier times, was the parade. When any of the leading parlor houses acquired a new girl possessing glamorous appeal, the madam would hire a smart looking coach and coachman, and drive up and down the avenues boldly exhibiting her latest addition to the flock. The madams were well-known and no one had to be told where the goods were available.

Seattle madam Lila Young.

In Seattle the parade went up and down Second Avenue, where Madams Lou Graham, Rae McRoberts, and Lila Young, among others, would show off their alluring new girls.

Spokane's Josey Tripp had two redheaded Creole girls from New Orleans. Josey would start out with these ladies in a fine coach, drawn by a team of spirited horses, and drive around town. It was quite a sight to see Josey and her two redheads driving down Riverside from the house on Post Street and proceed to the markets where everyone catered to her.

In Tacoma the promenade was made along Pacific Avenue, where Hattie Wickwire, Queen of Tacoma's Tenderloin, would ride at the head of her regular Saturday afternoon parade advertising the attractions of her establishment. The girls followed her in carriages down Pacific and up "C" Street to her place in Opera Alley.

Sometimes the madams, executives in the business of make-believe love, found the real article. Clara Dumont, who ran a popular sporting house in Seattle, was one of those who fell before the arrow of Cupid. Her true love was a young banker from San Francisco whose family did not cotton to the idea of him becoming seriously entangled with "one of those women." It was difficult for Clara and her banker to keep a low profile during their courtship, and it became impossible to do so after their betrothal—and her profession—was announced by a heartless press.

Rushing to tidy up her reputation as best she could, Clara sold her establishment three days before her marriage. Thus, the California banker did not marry a Seattle madam; she was an ex-madam of three days standing, a distinction that impressed neither family nor press.

Not all madams were as ready as Clara Dumont to give up their profitable careers for wedded bliss. Mabel Heath was not. Mabel was a widely known, pretty Portland courtesan in the late-1890s. As the proprietor of one of the most aristocratic houses in the city, she did a thriving business and lived in great style. She rode in a fine carriage, attended by a high-salaried coachman and several imported dogs. Mabel catered only to the moneyed interests in Portland and to important political leaders in the state.

According to Mabel's long-time maid, Sadie Harner, who was

Josey Tripp, one of Spokane's most well-known
madams, sat for this photograph in the spring of 1890.

This young lady, one of Josey Tripp's doves, smiles coyly as though she knows many of Spokane's secrets.

still living in Portland in the late-1940s, there was once a wealthy young man, a frequent caller at Mabel's place, whose business suddenly summoned him to Southern California permanently. Secretly, he was wildly infatuated with Mabel Heath, coyly holding her hand whenever he called and going through the motions of an 1890s romance.

It must be borne in mind that Mabel did not engage in the affairs to which her house was dedicated. A kiss on the cheek was the best a client ever received, and that only for a favored few.

Mabel's man had that longing look in his eyes, that nervousness of the bashful suitor with honest desires. He brought her flowers, which was like bringing a glass of water to a lake; he gave her a three-carat diamond ring even though she had one necklace alone worth well over $50,000. He gave

This is the only known photograph of Miss Mabel Heath, the Portland madam who did not follow her true love to California.

An Eastern Washington sporting house and its proprietress.

This shopworn old house is identified as "A Walla Walla bordello—1901."

her candy and he wrote love notes. Mabel was impressed and slowly her affection for him turned to love.

But the young man went to California. He wrote her a long letter inviting her south and promising wedding bells. Mabel replied saying she was tempted to accept his offer and that she also had feelings for him. However, she kept putting off the trip.

Finally, the lovesick wooer wrote to a newspaper friend in Portland, enclosing a copy of her letter and asking him to intercede. The newspaperman, later to become prominent in Portland, rushed to Mabel, putting in a strong plea for his friend.

He told the lovely madam that he had read a copy of her letter—it was charming, it was sentimental, it expressed returned love for his friend. What was the matter with her? Why did she not accept the offer?

The newspaperman, whom she respected, almost convinced her that romance was still the big thing in life. But she did not go.

Years later, when both she and the newspaperman were elder statesmen of their respective professions—though by then Mabel was retired—she told him she had often thought of her "lover" over the years, but that she had eventually lost track of him.

The newspaperman asked her to tell him the real reason she did not marry the young man if she had loved him. Mabel replied that her sweetheart had taken a terrible dislike to her profession and wanted her to quit after they were married. She could not make that sacrifice, she said, even for love.

Life was not all champagne and clam cakes and lovelorn suitors for the madams of the Pacific Northwest. Much of the rugged logging and mining country of Washington and Oregon in the last century made for tough, turbulent living conditions for women of any profession. Sometimes this unrestrained frontier life led to bullets.

Jennie Bright was one of the leading madams in Ruby City, a boisterous, booming silver-mining camp in Washington's Okanogan country. It was a raw-edged town where shootings were not infrequent and regard for law and order was not high on the list of community projects.

Old Ruby City, Washington Territory, pictured here in the only known photograph, was a lusty, boisterous silver mining camp called the "Babylon of the West." The girls of the line held forth in cabins shown at the top of the main street, and on the hillside at the top right of the photo.

At the edge of town, in a house well-known to the miners in the district, lived Jennie Bright and a number of young ladies. Shortly before a March dawn in 1888, one of Ruby City's more lecherous citizens, in a state of complete intoxication, attempted to force his way into Jennie's place. Greatly annoyed at being diverted from her business at such an hour, Jennie refused to permit him to enter. He then, according to reports, took a swing at Madam Bright. She then, not to miss having the last word on the doorstep of her own establishment, returned to her room for a revolver and shot the gentleman forthwith right through the heart, killing him instantly.

The man's body was found crumpled on the steps outside the house, and by the time the sheriff could be persuaded to inquire at the establishment for details of the incident, Madam Bright had time to board the stage for Spokane Falls, knowing that a few days later the whole affair would be forgotten in the heat of some new excitement in town. She then could, and did, return to her business unmolested by the law.

Legal entanglements always seemed to plague the madams, and not all law troubles arose from the nature of the business.

In 1888 one of the most luxurious and expensively furnished houses in Spokane was on lower Front Street (now Trent). Emblazoned over the front door was the name "Florence." When night fell, gentlemen with plenty of money in their pockets entered that door and received a warm welcome from the hostess. The girls were enticing, the wine good, and the music relaxing. Florence Crayman's place was, in a word, popular.

Florence was a shrewd businesswoman, running a profitable personal service business and saving a good deal of money. She had a large amount of capital invested in her house and furnishings, a large payroll, and an impressive bank balance. She also had good taste in sterling silver, of which she had accumulated a large variety. It was properly inventoried and she carried full insurance on it as well as her house and contents.

As some of the dash and flamboyance of Spokane's boom began to slide, a new mining boom to the north in British Columbia began to expand at a fast rate. Florence learned that the region badly needed just such a service as she ran, for which she could charge the heavy-pocketed miners more than twice the prices obtained in Spokane.

While the enterprising madam was considering the advantages of such a change of location, her house burned down. She at once put in a claim for the insurance money. But a few days later she was arrested by the U.S. Marshal for arson. It seemed that a saloon swamper named Crookedly Ike had confessed that he was paid $200 by Florence to set fire to her place, and that he had shipped all her silver up to Canada the day before the fire.

Ike's confession was made more plausible when it was learned that a day after the fire he had lost $200 in a poker game at Doc Brown's gambling house.

Indignant at such a ridiculous charge, Madam Florence hired Frank Graves to defend her. Sam Hyde, U.S. district attorney, was the prosecutor.

During the well-attended trial, Crookedly Ike told his story. Frank Graves, in a searching cross-examination, made Ike sound loathsome, but he could not destroy the effect of his testimony.

Then the prosecutor called Florence to the stand. On a table the bailiff set, one by one, the silver pieces supposedly lost in the fire. Hyde then asked Florence, "Madam, is this your silver?" Florence gave the silver one look, and exclaimed in a soft, innocent tone, "Why, yes, sir, it surely is. And how glad I am to see it again. I haven't seen it since that day when Crookedly Ike stole it and then set fire to my place to conceal his crime!"

Florence won. She collected both the insurance money and her precious silver, and moved to Canada where she continued as a mistress of her trade until well into this century.

Some of the surprising revelations brought to light during the lifetimes of the madams, and some known only after their passing, have added to the interest and mystery of these women.

Ruby Booth was a popular brothel keeper in Salem, Oregon, just prior to the turn of the century. When she died it was learned that her real name was Mary Scott Singleton, a member of a wealthy and respected Connecticut family and mother of two children; a daughter who was raised in the East and a son who graduated from Harvard.

Madam Mollie James of Astoria, Oregon, accumulated a small fortune and retired from the life to purchase and operate a traveling circus in the East. She was only twenty-five years old. Her circus was later acquired by P.T. Barnum.

Then there is the story of Spokane madam Julia Spencer and her protector, one Raymond T. Kressler. A buggy salesman, Raymond T. had been a favorite customer at Madam Spencer's house for some years. On a cold December morning, Kressler defended Julia Spencer's honor in a duel and thereafter became the good madam's live-in protector. This arrangement continued until Julia retired in her mid-thirties. She and Kressler then moved to a farm in Pennsylvania where they lived out their years.

Miss Winnie Gaylord ran brothels in Portland, Tacoma, and Seattle. She retired from madamship in Seattle when the

Astoria's Mollie James, pictured here, retired from madamship and bought a traveling circus on the East Coast.

Madam Winnie Gaylord, of Seattle, Tacoma, and Portland, willed $5,000 for the care of her two cats.

red-light district was closed in 1917. Remaining unmarried, Winnie made a grand tour of the world, including Japan, China, India, Egypt, and France. Her last stop was in London, where she was found dead in her hotel room. A will, written two years prior to her death, left $5,000 for the care of her two cats, Toby and Crystal. The balance of the estate went to family members; the largest part to three sisters and two brothers, all living in San Francisco. Also, $20,000 was placed in trust for a nine-year-old niece. Consisting chiefly of gold, diamonds, and real estate, Winnie Gaylord's worth at the time of her death amounted to over $500,000.

An offbeat sidebar to the Winnie Gaylord story is the tale of the mysterious customer. In the mid-1890s, during the time Winnie was operating an elegant house on Seattle's Beacon Hill, she had a regular client with a strange inclination. This middle-aged man would appear several mornings a week at Winnie's house carrying a bundle which contained a complete outfit of women's clothing. He donned the garments and then he swept and dusted the brothel from cellar to attic. His work completed, he resumed his proper attire and departed, leaving a silver dollar on the parlor table. No one but Madam Gaylord ever knew his name. And she kept his secret.

As in any profession, madamship often had its lighter side. In Washington's Port Townsend, for example, there is the story of Madam Lottie Sinnott and the meat and fowl merchant.

Lottie Sinnott ran one of Port Townsend's leading 1890s brothels. Unlike the small houses along Water Street which served the sailors, loggers, and soldiers, Lottie's high-class "female boarding house" was located back against the bluff in the vicinity of today's Memorial Field. She catered to ship captains and mates and those upper class businessmen who cared to venture down from The Hill, as the "good" part of town was called.

Now Lottie had pride in her establishment and knew she was an economic force in the community, no matter what the ladies on The Hill thought of her. Merchants welcomed her business and were quick to grant favors, such as extending credit to her girls, for they knew Lottie was good for the payment.

Lottie, too, was one to grant favors to her valued customers, for she was selective and careful to offer the services of her

This is believed to be a photograph of Port
Townsend's Lottie Sinnott, who had difficulties with a
certain "meat and fowl" merchant.

house only to those of means. After all, she was not a Water Street girl. That is why, on one particular evening, she did not hesitate to extend the warmth of her house to three young men who had no money. One of the budding bon vivants, she knew, was the son of a dealer in meat and fowl in the town. Lottie had met the father, though he was not a client, and she was anxious to curry his favor, no doubt with the idea of establishing some little arrangement whereby she and her girls could avail themselves of the freshest and choicest of his products.

Thus, when the young man told her that he did not exactly have any present means of payment, but his father had guaranteed to make good the cost of an evening of first instructions and comfort for the son and his two cousins by Lottie and her boarders, she believed him. It would have been well, however, for Madam Sinnott to have taken note of the fact that the three young men had evidently bolstered their courage for the night's festivities with the consumption of a fair quantity of ardent spirits.

The proper instruction of a young man into the ways of painted ladies takes great care and patience, particularly if he is under the glow of drink. It is time consuming, and as someone once said, probably a madam, "time is money." By the time the instruction was finished and the young men were sent back into the world wiser and happier than they had thought possible, the bill for the three amounted to a not insignificant sum.

Lottie waited for some communication from the father regarding payment, but nothing immediately came. A couple of weeks passed with still no word from the meat and fowl merchant, and Lottie decided to politely advance her cause. She drafted a courteously worded letter to the father, taking great care not to offend, requesting him to satisfy the charges accumulated by his son and nephews. The letter was delivered to his place of business on The Hill.

The next day Lottie received a letter from the meat and fowl merchant. The letter, to the good madam's chagrin, was a rambling stream of abuse, directed at her for even attempting a low, morally-deficient, cruel, criminal thing such as blackmailing him for something that, if it occurred at all, he had no part of nor the slightest knowledge of. Lottie was, to say the least, taken aback.

Gathering herself, Lottie wrote another letter as a peace-keeping gesture, and sent it to The Hill. Again, a reply of rebuke was sent back to her.

Lottie Sinnott then made a small mistake, her judgment clouded no doubt by pride and righteous anger. She let it be known among her acquaintances in the mercantile trade that a certain dealer in meat and fowl was not to be trusted in business, and that included his family as well.

One day, while Lottie and her boarders were out shopping, an unknown miscreant entered her house and left in that noble establishment several dozen, live, excited, bowel-loosened chickens. At least, that's how they tell it in Port Townsend.

Ingenuity, as any small business owner knows, often is the difference between growth and stagnation. Fannie Cardwell was an ingenious madam whose base of operations in the 1890s was the lively lumber and fishing port of Marshfield (now Coos Bay), on Oregon's central coast. Her "offices" were in a

This was Front Street, Marshfield, Oregon, in the 1890s. Madam Fannie Cardwell operated out of the rooms next to the large flag (left center). The first building on the right also housed nymphs of the night in rooms over a grocery store.

building on Front Street in the center of Marshfield's business district.

Marshfield in those days was a rowdy, free-spending town that catered to the needs of droves of loggers and seamen who tarried there for rest and recreation. Indeed, the "R&R" services were a major feature in the economic health of the town. One old-timer described the main thoroughfare, Front Street, as consisting of "alternately saloons and houses of prostitution, interposed with some businesses."

Every Saturday night Front Street was alive and business for Fannie Cardwell was good. But it was during the several-times-a-year logger's holidays that Marshfield really exploded. Around the Fourth of July, at Christmas, and usually one additional time during the year, a multitude of woods-weary loggers would descend on Marshfield for a full week of rest and recreation. As soon as they hit town they would get a bath and a shave, then they would head for the saloons and the girls.

Now Fannie Cardwell was a public-spirited business owner who wanted to help assure the economic well-being of Marshfield, and one way to do that, she figured, was to enlarge her business. But there was a problem with that noble desire: where to obtain additional rooms? There were only so many suitable places on Front Street and the immediate area, and they were taken up by Fannie's competitors. If she moved too far away from Front Street she stood to lose customers to contemporaries because of her remote location.

Fannie used her ingenuity to solve this typical small-business quandary. The waterfront, with all its docks and piers and moorages, ran parallel to the rear of the buildings on the east side of Front Street. Fannie arranged for the purchase of seven small houseboats or "float houses," as they were called then, and moored them close to her main establishment. By the time of the next logger's holiday week she was ready, and her business doubled. When the week was over she had her float houses towed to the south end of the bay where they rested until the next onslaught.

The press and Front Street regulars referred to Madam Cardwell's houseboats as "Fannie's Flotilla." The good people of the town no doubt had other names for them.

This was Celia Levi, a Marshfield, Oregon (Coos Bay), working girl who held forth on Front Street in 1892.

Ingenuity also helped another madam, Mabel Cox, with a problem of a different kind. Mabel operated an Oregon sporting house in the Douglas County community of Roseburg in the late 1890s. Her place was on the east side of Main Street, between Douglas and Washington. On the north side of Mabel's house was the Van Houten Hotel, and adjoining her on the other side was a large livery stable. Across the street was another hotel and several businesses.

Mabel's problem was that her house, particularly the walkway leading to the front door, was too visible for the comfort of many would-be customers. She was losing business to several other brothels around town that were not quite so convenient to prying eyes. Something had to be done.

The answer came in the form of a high board fence that the resourceful madam constructed all the way around the house. A sort of baffle, located within the yard at the main opening in the fence, prevented passers-by from looking up the walk to the front door. Customers could then simply duck quickly into the fence opening, go around the baffle, and feel protected from view. Mabel's place became known as "The Stockade," and "The High Board."

The ingenious madam later cut an inconspicuous door in the rear of the house so that her shy clients could enter and leave by way of the stables next door and avoid the front entrance entirely. It was said by old-timers in Roseburg that some of the regular customers using the rear door included two city councilmen, a deputy sheriff, and a minister.

And then there was Madam Lou Graham.

Of all the successful and popular madams in the Pacific Northwest, none stood out with more personality, grace, savvy, or political clout than did a five-foot-two-inch, blue-eyed, German-born lass whose real name was Dorothea Georgine Emile Ohben. She was known to all as Lou Graham of Seattle.

Madam Lou stepped daintily down the gangplank of the steamer *Pacific Pride* in February 1888. She was twenty-seven-years-old and had come north to seek her fortune. Her years as an active member of San Francisco's Barbary Coast had provided a wealth of experience in her trade and she was ready to put it to use in the booming, boisterous city on Puget Sound.

Shortly after Lou arrived in Seattle she approached the city's top business leaders with an idea that matched her ambition. Seattle was in the process of trying to attract new business—big business. Efforts were being made to get a transcontinental rail connection, and the shipping and lumber industries were growing with the promise of making Seattle a world port. The controlling interests in town wanted Seattle to become a real city with all the wealth and acclaim that went with it.

But there was a problem, as Lou Graham pointed out to the business leaders. There was no place in town classy enough to cater to the rest and recreation needs of the top-hat and black-tie set. If Seattle was to entice industry moguls from the Eastern and Mid-Western urban centers, there would have to be a facility available for them to enjoy an evening of comfort and relaxation in an atmosphere of good music, fine wine, and the company of beautiful, intelligent, amenable ladies.

Such an enterprise would need to have the opulence and class of similar facilities around New York, Chicago, San

The main parlor in Lou Graham's place was sumptuous. The large chairs shown in this photo were for the comfort of client's; the small chair in the center was where a girl would demurely wait.

Francisco, Paris, and London. It would have to be staffed with lovely, talented, understanding hostesses imported from all over the world. It would need ladies who were comfortable in discussing affairs of the nation and the globe, as well as the arts and "personal" matters.

Since the beginning of civilization, man had acknowledged the need for proper entertainment and consideration of visiting dignitaries. Seattle had a number of fine parlor houses, to be sure, and countless brothels of varying degrees of style and class south of Yesler, but none were of the magnitude suggested by Lou Graham.

To further instill in the city fathers a sense of confidence and sincerity in her plan, Lou proposed that she would adhere to a strict and fair price index, not charging all that the traffic would bear as did her peers. She would guarantee honesty in all her dealings and would assure the safety, anonymity, and satisfaction of all guests.

She was also willing to pay her fair share into city coffers, which amount, she explained, would add a significant sum to the treasury. In return, Lou asked only that she be allowed to operate her place of hospitality freely and unmolested.

The business leaders were impressed. They agreed that an enterprise such as proposed by Lou Graham would make a genuine contribution to the economic growth of the city. And Lou obviously had the intelligence, experience, the regal bearing and business acumen to pull it off.

When could she start?

Lou's place was on the southwest corner of Third Avenue South and Washington Street. It was a sumptuous multi-level house that was first-class in every respect. Her girls were recruited from among the best houses world-wide, and included French, English, and Oriental courtesans. The plush furnishings and able staff drew compliments from wealthy patrons, who likened Lou's place to the finest establishments of its kind in the world.

It was Lou's permanent policy that highly placed representatives in the city government would be served at no cost, any time of the day or night. It was said that more city business was transacted at Lou's place than at City Hall (which was only a block away).

Lou ran a clean house and never had a bit of trouble, except for the usual breakage, several heart attacks by over-eager elderly clients, and a favorite police official who accidentally shot a settee while showing off his gun. And there was the time the shipping magnate's son set fire to Lou's place one New Year's Eve. The fire did not amount to much and the family paid for the drapes, the wallpaper, and Mary Anne's dress.

It cost Lou a fortune to build and furnish her house, with its red velvet draperies and hand-painted tables. In Madam Graham's own room reposed a large ornate gold bed with hangings of lace. Statues and other imported art gave every room a touch of elegance. Lou boasted that her house had all the convenience of home, and a lot more fun. She had a strict rule that no client would ever hear foul language in her house—not a word he would not want used before his wife and children.

For those honored clients with the fare to stay overnight, special services were provided. The next morning the guest rose to find his shirt freshly laundered and starched, suit pressed, and breakfast ready. If he were particularly well off, or a highly placed politician, the client could take over the house for the night and invite his friends. The price was high. Lou extended credit, and a customer properly vouched for or known could run up a large bill. Like most of the high ranking madams, Lou could check with banker friends and get a credit line on anybody.

Madam Lou Graham amassed a fortune through her "civic-minded" enterprise. She became a big landholder in the Northwest, and invested profitably in gold, diamonds, and stocks. After the devastating Seattle fire in June 1889, Lou was able immediately to purchase additional property and rebuild. Her new structure, at the same location, was a beautiful brick and stone building even more palatial than the original. She also built a mansion where she lived during her private hours, on East Madison Street and Twenty-first Avenue. Lou's private home stood until 1966; her "house" still stands at Third

This was a room in Madam Lou Graham's elegant establishment. The photo shows examples of the fine detail work and art which made Lou's parlor house a showplace for distinguished Seattle visitors.

and Washington and is now the offices of the Washington State Trial Lawyer's Association.

The big brick pleasure house was well-known, as was its proprietress, all along the Pacific Coast. It became a regular stop for the trolley cars. In the evening, if there were no women on the trolley, the conductor would shout: "All out for Lou Graham's place!"

One of Lou's passions and long standing habits was her weekly afternoon carriage ride around town. Dressed in their finest attire, Madam Lou and several of her newest ladies would be driven up and down the streets of the main business district. Friends would call out to Lou, and she would wave or blow a kiss. It was a high point in her week to get out and be seen. The ride invariably ended at the Bon Marche or Frederick and Nelson or some small, exclusive jewelry or dress shop, where Lou and her girls would pick out whatever finery or jewelry appealed to them, and charge it to her account.

There is a Lou Graham story that begs to be told, and to the day she died she claimed it was true. There was a room in Lou's place which was the color of that metal that makes hearts jump. Everything that glittered in the Gold Room may not have been the precious metal itself, but the gold-rimmed goldfish bowls and the shiny cuspidors and the bright chandeliers were eighteen-carat, without doubt.

Every year the room was done over in gold-leaf and every day it was polished like the brass handles of the big front door. One time, soon after the yearly going over, a guest accidentally leaned against a panel while the gilt was still soft. The next day Lou told a painter, "Come with me and I'll show you where a man put his hand last night."

"If it's all the same to you, Miss Graham," replied the shy workman, "I'd rather have a glass of beer."

Another story concerns a visit to Lou's place by a priest. Our Lady of Good Help Catholic Church, built in the late 1860s, stood on the northeast corner of Third Avenue South and Washington Street. Diagonally across the street was the sin palace of Madame Lou Graham. For some years there was an uneasy coexistence of piety and prostitution at the same intersection.

One day in 1890, one of Lou's doves was seriously ill.

Madam Lou Graham's famous sporting house still
stands at the corner of Third Avenue South and
Washington in Seattle. It is now the home of the
Washington State Trial Lawyers Association.

Fearing the worst, and knowing the girl was Catholic, Lou sent
across the street for a priest. Father Prefontaine came quickly
over for spiritual consolation. After visiting the sick girl for
some time, the good Father waited while she was bundled off to
the hospital.

Preparing to go back across the street, the compassionate
priest was asked by one of the other girls to hear her
confession before he left. They went into the parlor and when
they came out a short while later, the fallen angel was
beaming. Another girl made the same request, then another.
Before Father Prefontaine left Lou's place, he heard the
confessions of over a dozen of the ladies. Only two of them
were Catholic.

Lettie Stillwell graced the house of Madam Lou
Graham in the early 1890s. A favorite of many
wealthy clients, Lettie went on to operate her own fine
house in Missoula, Montana.

Afterward Lou said the church of Our Lady of Good Help increased its Sunday attendance by several because of that visit. And those new devotees did not have far to walk.

Lou Graham was the darling of The Establishment, and she reveled in her position. She returned the generosity the city had shown her by contributing heavily to a wide variety of city-sponsored projects and charities. She made loans of thousands of dollars to business friends, not all of which was ever recovered, particularly during the depression of 1893.

When Lou passed away in 1903 at the early age of forty-three, she left in her will what amounted to the largest single cash endowment to a civic program ever seen in the history of Seattle. She bequeathed a quarter of a million dollars to the King County schools.

After she died, Lou's gold bed was acquired by Hiram C. Gill, lawyer for most of the turn of the century brothel keepers, and later mayor of Seattle. Rumors have persisted to this day, though without much proof, that the great gold bed of Madam Lou Graham is still active in the service of Venus, and that the imprints of many a legislator, judge, city councilman, shipping magnate, and respected society patron have been made on the ornate old relic.

When Lou Graham walked down the gangplank that February day in 1888, she was ready to own Seattle. She almost did.

CHAPTER THREE
The Girls

The doves brought comfort
  To the roughness o' pioneer life.
The softness and frills o' the bawdy house
  Took the edge off o' some o' the strife.

—Old Western Doggerel

They came to the Pacific Northwest from all points on the globe, often arriving with light baggage and new names; girls who followed their trade in the rugged mining camps and logging settlements and new, booming cities. They were Annie, Lillie, Ella, Mattie, Kittie, Pearl, Blanche, and Ruby. They went by nicknames such as: Wild Rose, French Rita, and Velvet Bon. One girl of the line in Baker City, Oregon, was known only as Black Cat.

Some of the girls were products of surprisingly well-to-do families. Most of them, though, were of more ordinary or even austere backgrounds who chose or fell into the profession for a wide range of reasons. It was a tough career choice and although there were certainly lighter moments, none of the girls were the always cheerful, laughing, golden-hearted coquettes depicted in movies.

The quality of life, experiences, and environments of the soiled doves of the Northwest, as elsewhere, varied greatly. For example, consider the profiles of Francoise DuMonet and Ella Monroe.

One afternoon in the spring of 1887, when the steamer *Queen of the Pacific* tied up at the Ocean Dock at the foot of Seattle's Main Street, there stepped down a mystery. She was young, apparently about twenty-two years of age. She was

This lady was known in various Oregon and
Washington mining camps as "French Rita." The
photograph was taken by Seattle photographer S.
Patton, which may indicate that the comely miss was
known "Down on the Sawdust" as well.

French and, according to one who knew, "pretty, dark-eyed,
fresh-faced." Her attire was as stylish as any woman cared to
be when traveling by ship through the chill fog of Puget Sound
waters.

By all precedent, she should have done one of two things:
been met by a husband, relative or friend; or inquired the way
to one of the saloons in The District. She did neither. She
checked into Seattle's principal hotel, the Washington, where
she remained in seclusion, taking her meals alone, seeing no
one.

Conjecture spread through the better drinking emporiums
and men's clubs about the lone, beautiful lady with the bearing
of nobility. Whispered rumors abounded, eyebrows and
questions were raised. Her name was known before anything

else; she had signed the hotel register as Francoise DuMonet. Her background was to remain mysterious, but not the next year of her future. For Mlle. DuMonet was Seattle's first high-class, high-priced working girl.

She only lingered in Seattle one year and not much remains to record her life there. It is known that lovely Francoise always worked alone and was never seen in the lower establishments south of Yesler. She was not affiliated with any parlor house in town, nor did she make friends with others in the trade. She preferred to keep to herself when not working, seldom leaving her room.

Her method was to become acquainted with selected wealthy

This was popular "Velvet Bon" of Aurora, a wild gold mining settlement in Baker County, Oregon. Many of the sporting girls were known only by their nicknames, their true names having been discarded along the way.

businessmen and highly placed city leaders. Those liaisons led to regular and substantial deposits by Francoise in the Dexter Horton Bank.

Hauntingly fascinating, she remained a mystery for men to contemplate. She could have established herself as a successful, perhaps famous madam, but that was not her way. And in a year she was gone, to the disheartenment of certain Seattle men. Some said she went back to Paris, but it could have been Kansas City or San Francisco or New Orleans. In any event, she was never again seen in Seattle.

At the same time that Francoise DuMonet was holding forth with Seattle's money men in fine hotels, Ella Monroe was working out of a line crib in the gold camp of Loomis in Washington's Okanogan country. Ella was not beautiful, but in a rugged district of few women she and her sisters in the trade did a good business. Ella lived simply, her needs few. She, too, stayed indoors most of the time, but unlike Francoise, her accommodations were far from first-class. Her clients were unkempt, rowdy miners, not polished or gentlemanly civic leaders.

And within a year, Ella, too, was gone. But, again unlike Francoise, it is doubtful anyone really cared, her place on the line being taken up immediately by another.

Two women, working at the same point in time in a profession that was the same yet different; two lives, similar and dissimilar.

Many of the girls of the trade who found their way to the Pacific Northwest were the same ladies who gave colorful notoriety to the Barbary Coast and the Klondike. By many names they were known. Lillie Vaughn for example—by her own admission—called herself Kittie Beaumont when she resided on Sacramento Street in San Francisco in 1884. She was May Brown two years later in Portland, and the next year "Lillie-Kittie-May" was known as Mary Chambers in Seattle, where she listed her employment when arrested as "seamstress." At one point, in the late 1880s and 1890s, there were so many "seamstresses" in Seattle that it should have been the center of the Northwest garment industry.

Stories about the Northwest's sporting girls abound in musty records of the day and in reminiscences of long gone

This unidentified Portland red-light girl strikes a
curtsy pose for the photographer.

old-timers. Once rooted out the tales offer an entertaining, sometimes poignant, look at the practitioners of a pioneer industry not often detailed in histories of Oregon and Washington.

As noted earlier, some of the bawdy belles in the Pacific Northwest have been identified as coming from families whose wealth and position would seem to preclude such a career choice by any of its members. But it did occur from time to time that a damsel from such a family chose, for some mysterious reason, to follow the scarlet path. Take the case of Lady X from Seattle.

This particular lady shall have to remain nameless for her family is even to this day part of Seattle society. She was a wealthy, cultured woman in her mid-thirties, married to a man of an old-line family. A couple of years before the turn of the century, Mrs. X took leave of home and husband to, as many thought, travel abroad with a female companion. To the very great surprise of her friends, and the deep chagrin of her family, it was discovered a month or so later, quite by accident, that her travels took her only a little south of Yesler Way—into the very heart of the red-light district.

It seems that the husband of one of Lady X's friends occasionally stepped south of Yesler to conduct personal research of some nature. One evening, this wandering swain happened into the parlor of a certain house marked by a porch lamp's crimson glow. Though not specifically recorded, his shocked remarks must have been interesting when the madam of the house brought out for his approval her new addition, none other than the Europe-visiting matron, Lady X.

The story ends with a quiet divorce in two leading Seattle families, and a certain lady moving to San Francisco. It is a mystery whether she continued in her new profession or whether she kept that part of her past to herself, perhaps remarrying—maybe into San Francisco society.

The subject of marriages by nymphs of the night is central to a wealth of stories in the Northwest. The fact that the girls in the trade sometimes married their customers should be no surprise, for Cupid's arrows are surely not restricted to only those who practice the moral professions. Let us cite the romantic escapade of Miss Louise DuPuy.

In its heyday, the wild and open gold camp of Canyon City, in Eastern Oregon's John Day country, had its share of girls of the line. The miners working their rich placers in Whiskey Gulch and the heavy-veined hillside mines of the area brought a continued supply of nuggets and dust to the purses of the appreciative and ever-so-friendly ladies.

One of these fair ones was Mademoiselle Louise DuPuy, a lovely French-accented girl who had really been no closer to Paris than St. Louis. It mattered not that her *oui-oui* was perhaps less than natural, the miners along the Gulch loved her. And Mlle. Louise ruled their hearts—and their gold dust pokes—with a feminine charm that made drunkards sober and sober men mellow.

On a day in 1869, when it was discovered that the lovely Louise was not receiving callers, indeed was not even present in her small cottage, the tale spread through the mines and saloons that a miner had stolen her during the night and spirited her away against her wishes.

A furious posse of "lovers" was quickly made up, but they had no place to go as no one knew where the bedeviled miscreant had taken her. After searching randomly through the district for a week, the would-be rescuers of the fair Louise learned the awful truth—the couple had been married in the mining settlement of Dixie (now Prairie City). The posse was dismissed.

In Portland, the gentle ties of wedlock saved Sophie Knight from the clutches of the law. Her 1889 prostitution case was dismissed and a court notation next to her name stated: "Married and living a better life."

From the gold mining settlement of Nighthawk in Washington's Similkameen Valley up near the Canadian border, comes this sad tale of hopeless love. A certain young miner became infatuated with a certain young businesswoman who lived in a cabin at the edge of town.

The more he saw her the deeper grew his affection, until he reached that profound state of unswerving, immeasurable, true love. Unfortunately, the young lovelorn miner was not as successful at his profession as the lady was at hers. His claim showed only mediocre results, the product of which found its way to the silk purse of the young lady at the edge of town.

Interior view of a nineteenth century Oregon gold camp red-light cabin.
The facilities were often basic for the girls of the line.

The miner wanted to marry his shady lady. But although she did have feelings for him—more than for the others, anyway—hers was a successful and growing business and she could not see the logic in reversing her fortunes at that particular time. If only he would strike it rich, then she might agree to retire to a life of wedded bliss.

He pleaded, she spurned; he begged, she disdained; he wheedled, she rejected. Finally, steeped in the bottomless chasm of unrequited love, the dispirited miner took his life with his trusty .44.

Soon after that tragic day the young miner's partner struck the vein that surely would have solved his lady's quandary.

That's the way the story goes in Nighthawk.

The ladies often came from varied and unusual backgrounds. In Aberdeen there once worked a nymph who had been a circus rider in Spain. And Ada James, a pretty strumpet who worked at Irish Moll's place in The Dalles, was reputed to have been a well-known and respected Union nurse in the Civil War. If true, her nursing practice certainly took a more personal turn on the banks of the Columbia River than it did in the army hospitals of the East.

Then there is the fascinating tale of Florence and Fannie Bloom, sisters who practiced their trade in the early 1860s in the gold camp of Clarksville, near the Burnt River placer diggings in Oregon's Baker County.

That they were truly sisters is probably as much a fact as that their real names were Florence and Fannie Bloom; not much chance of either. In any case, the girls set up shop in a large tent with board sides and a dirt floor. They partitioned off "rooms," got a stove, a table, some chairs, and two beds, and announced the opening of a new enterprise in Clarksville.

Business was good for the accommodating Bloom sisters. Their position near the placers allowed them first chance at the boys heading to town. When the miners cleaned up their long-tom sluices and rockers, the Bloom girls cleaned up on the miners.

One day, while raking and sweeping the "floor," one of the ladies noticed what appeared to be a piece of gold. The chunk she picked up was exactly that, and it was not the only one. The excited girls moved out the furniture and panned the floor.

The Bloom sisters of Clarksville, Oregon, appear to
be in high spirits after striking it rich at their
"boardinghouse."

Before the day was over they had $500. They were, quite
literally, sitting on a gold mine. Florence and Fannie staked a
claim to their floor and the immediate vicinity and sold the
claim. The story goes that one of them returned to the East and
told her folks that her "boardinghouse" venture in Oregon had
been very successful.

Tales of buried treasure have not escaped connection with
the shady ladies of the Northwest. In the ranching town of
Burns, in Oregon's magnificent high desert country of Harney
County, there lived a lady who around 1900 made the cowboys'
stay in town especially joyful.

Though this dove died early of one malady or another—a too
frequent occurrence in the small towns of an earlier age—she
was supposed to have left behind a legacy of sorts. For this

A Seattle parlor house girl.

careful nymph, with a view toward independence and trusting only herself, was reputed to have secreted somewhere in the house, or around the house, or in the shed, or around the shed, a substantial sum in gold coin—proceeds acquired from her many appreciative cowboy friends.

The lady's house still stands in Burns, though the shed itself is gone. But certainly any serious thoughts of hidden gold coins should be paid no mind. And if, perchance, the authors are observed absently poking about a certain old house, they should not be paid any mind, either.

The sporting girls as a group knew how to have fun. That is not to say theirs was a light-hearted, pleasant profession, because it most certainly was not. But in their line of work, which was often less than agreeable, efforts to bring amusement through games and pranks were noteworthy events. There are enough accounts of spirited pranks and mischievous frolicsome stunts that we can know with certainty that the ladies of comfort and joy did, in fact, know how to have fun. Any allegation to the contrary is so much flapdoodle.

As a case in point, take the "Longest Beard" game as played in Lila Young's Seattle parlor house.

Early in the week, when business was less brisk, the nymphs would make a pool, each contributing one dollar. It was not the amount but the fun involved that made the game a success.

The winner took all. And the winner was the lassie who had snared the man with the longest beard. Sometimes, in the enthusiasm of the competition, a would-be customer with a close shave did not have a chance with any of the girls involved in the game until the pool was won. One would hope that Madam Young kept one or two girls in reserve to solace those beardless chaps while the game was going forth.

Never was a parlor contest more spirited or laugh provoking. Often a siren, popular among the stable of bearded lads, would lose the stakes because from laughter she was unable to measure her companion's whiskers. The expression, "he's my jockey," meaning the favored choice in any sort of competition, is said to have originated at the whiskers game in Lila Young's parlor house. The phrase is still heard from time to time in Seattle. Jockey was the sly word the girls used as they escorted a possible winner up the stairs to a boudoir, thus calling attention to their selection in case there was doubt later as to the length of the man's beard. The male players usually never suspected their important roles in this hilarious pastime.

The girls had rulers in their rooms with which to measure the face-pieces, paving the way toward the actual calculation with such remarks as: "Daddy has such a lovely beard. Mind if Tootsie measures it? Tootsie loves long beards." After the beard measuring, the principal business was conducted.

One of the girls was chosen as scorekeeper. Only one chance was allowed each girl. The winner was given a rousing cheer after which the evening progressed along the usual lines.

Occasionally one of the girls would arrange for the appearance of a false-bearded friend sporting extraordinarily long whiskers. If caught, the mischievous damsel had to buy champagne for the house.

This small brothel in Salem, Oregon, catered to laboring men. Though the state capitol was just a few blocks away, the government leaders who chose to dally with sporting girls doubtless sought their comfort elsewhere than this modest little house.

"Tacoma May" operated and worked in a number of
brothels in Washington. At one time she ran a house
in Tacoma for Boss Sport Harry Morgan.

Sporting girls were not over-modest, to say the least, and
when they participated in attention getting stunts they were
usually done in a saucy, flamboyant style.

On a warm evening in September 1892, three of Portland's
daughters of joy, possibly moved by the boredom of the slow
night, staged an impromptu nude dance on the wooden
sidewalk in front of their Davis Street bordello. A crowd
naturally convened to appreciate the art and grace of the
dance, and among the culture lovers were officers of the police.

The three dancing nymphs were summarily fined in police
court, according to the *Morning Oregonian*, for "naughty
capers."

At least those three were probably safer in their stunt than
were the two lady horse racers in Baker City. On the Fourth of
July in 1872, Lillie Mack and a girl named Alice, both local
"businesswomen," decided to engage in a horse race down the
main street as their contribution to the day's festivities. As
they were provided with white horses for the event, the girls

thought it somehow appropriate to wear white dresses.

At the starter's pistol shot, the lady jockeys raced up the street, hair and white dresses no doubt flying in the wind as they coaxed their white chargers to victory. Men and little boys cheered them on, the good ladies ignored them. It was all part of the spirit of the holiday, and damned fine advertising for their house.

The results? Hard to tell. Lillie's horse collided with a buggy and Alice's mount ran up a side street, according to the *Bedrock Democrat.* Maybe it was a draw.

It was not unusual for sporting girls to take part in Fourth of July activities—that spirited American holiday was always marked by lively, noisy events and festivities. It was in keeping with the rollicking, free and easy way of the shady ladies. Independence Day was a time for the local working girls to show their independence, too.

It was in that spirit that three bawdy belles from a Salem, Oregon, sporting house took part in a Willamette River Fourth of July race just after the turn of the century. The entry represented by Mary Koning, Edith Jerman, and Maud Vaughn did not come close to winning, but the frolicsome trio had a loyal and tumultuous cheering section.

Such family and religious holidays as Christmas and Easter, however, did not draw the ladies out into public stunts or displays. But Christmas was celebrated in many sporting houses just as it was in other American homes. In 1905, the girls working out of Olympia's Kneeland Hotel, at Fourth and Main, entered into the Christmas holidays in a different and festive way. They all took to wearing a special "Santa's little helper" outfit as their working attire: long red silk nighties trimmed in white lace and fur, red slippers with tiny bells, and red velvet caps. The jolly old fellow himself may have paused awhile at the Kneeland on that special Christmas Eve.

Innovation and novelty added spice and originality to the profession. Whether in Ruby City, Jacksonville, or Seattle, customers loved to see something different and new. And in the competitive pleasure business, the girl who could bring a fresh, unconventional spark to the game, either in appearance or practice, stood out from her more prosaic sisters.

One of Lou Graham's most popular girls was a sweet, gentle

young lady named Carrie Belle. Carrie had dark hair and eyes, and a great fondness for the color white. The rugs in her boudoir were white, the coverlet on her bed was white, and the draperies were white. She loved white roses. When you went to see Carrie the atmosphere was angelic—up to a point. A well-known present day Seattle attorney has three of Carrie Belle's ornate white fans.

In Portland's North End it was an eye-catching novelty to see some of the girls riding bicycles through the streets, throwing out teasing remarks—along with their addresses—to interested male pedestrians.

And in the wild gold camp of Cornucopia, high in the mountains of northeastern Oregon, a well-endowed red-light girl, known only as Blue Stockings, used to play a gold nugget game with the fellows. Wearing a low-cut bodice guaranteed to display her natural charms, Blue Stockings would spot miners paying for their drinks with gold, and call out to them: "Toss 'em, boys, toss 'em." She would then bend forward as a laughing miner flicked tiny gold nuggets toward her. She kept the ones she could catch between her ample bosoms. The additional benefit of the game to Blue Stockings was that after a few nuggets were tossed, her dexterous chest so excited the boys that she soon had all the business she wanted for the night.

Another innovative dove was one whose name has been lost but who worked out of Madam Lida Fanshaw's Mansion of Sin in Portland in the 1890s. This talented lady could play the piano and sing in a particularly erotic husky voice. She gave customers a treat by improvising short bawdy songs about them. It was a mark of distinction among Portland rakes to have been the subject of a ribald ditty at Madam Fanshaw's.

It was important in the pleasure business to cater to the special needs and requests of customers. It was, after all, a highly competitive profession. The guiding byword was: "Anything you like, Mister, any way you like it." The same sexual deviations spoken of in hushed tones today were spoken of even more quietly in the 1800s, but they were indeed present. The twentieth century does not have an exclusive claim on kinkiness; the subject was just not as open in those days.

Emma Lane, a Spokane sporting girl in the early
1900s, shows her modest side, except for the large
gemstone set in her silver bracelet.

A Pacific Northwest gold camp girl.

"Frances," pictured here, was a Portland North End
girl in 1911.

From Rae McRoberts' sumptuous parlor house in Seattle
comes the story of elderly "Uncle Ned." Often the most sober
clients had the strangest quirks, proving perhaps that alcohol
cannot be called the sole cause for going bizarre. Uncle Ned
did not drink. Uncle Ned liked sleighs. He really liked sleighs.

Once every winter for some years, usually after Seattle's
first good snowfall, Uncle Ned would arrange with Madam Rae
for the exclusive use of the house for one night. The fee was
reportedly astronomical, especially for those days: $2,000.
Even allowing for exaggeration, it was doubtless a pricey
evening of fun.

The agreement was that all activities on that special night be directed in his behalf. Madam Rae knew precisely what he wanted and preparations were made.

The evening began in the music parlor, where Ned was seated in a comfortable chair in the middle of the room. All of the girls would assemble around him, except one lass who was at the piano. They would then sing to him, caressing his hair, face, and bony frame, establishing that he was the center of their attention. Oh yes, the girls were all nude. And Ned was fully clothed.

It was Ned's night and anything went.

Having enjoyed his exhilarating warm-up by the girls, he was now ready for his particular thrill. He was led by a procession of naughty nymphs into another parlor where in the center of the dimmed room sat a small one-horse sleigh. Ned would take a seat in the sleigh and, with the voice of authority, order two buckets of chopped ice, demanding that the pieces not be over two inches square. The ice, having been previously prepared, was promptly deposited on the front floorboards of the sleigh at his feet.

Two girls, one at each side, requested permission to remove Ned's shoes and clothes, to which he agreed. During the undressing interlude the gentle strains of *Jingle Bells* (*The One-Horse Open Sleigh*) was played softly on the piano in the next room. A girl approached Ned with a small leather belt of jingling bells which she placed in his hand.

He then began shaking the jingle bells, the piano picked up the tempo, and Uncle Ned plunged his feet into the pile of ice on the floor of the sleigh. At this exact time, with Ned vigorously and gleefully rattling his bells, and the piano playing *Jingle Bells* in fortissimo, the girls began to give Uncle Ned very precise personal service—he still seated in the sleigh, with feet in ice—until he achieved that which was the primary reason for any visit to any brothel.

Poor old Uncle Ned, satiated and exhausted, would then thank the girls and shout: "There is nothing equal to a good sleigh ride!" He was then put to bed to sleep it off.

That's a story they tell about Rae McRoberts' house.

Not all of the Northwest gentlemen knew how to deal with the naughty ladies. The doves were not a universal draw to all males—many shy or godly or married were not interested in

Mattie Coleman, one of Rae McRoberts' nymphs of
the night, may have helped with Uncle Ned's sleigh
ride.

dallying with the ladies of ultimate accessibility. On occasion
the unexpected occurred—sometimes humorously—when these
fellows met up with the girls. For example, there was the
episode of Pearl Lorry's plum pudding.

Pearl Lorry was a successful lady of the evening from
England who practiced her profession in Portland. Her "office"
in 1893 was a small house up at Seventeenth and Couch in the
North End.

Jonathan Timmons ran a jewelry and clock shop in
downtown Portland, and it was Pearl's custom to make most of

Dora Clark, left, and Maud Morrison were partners for four years in an
early 1900s Portland sporting house, located at Sixth and Stark.

her glittery purchases from him. Jeweler Timmons was a respectable man, a church-goer, and father of three children. But he was nonetheless impressed by the gentle manners and polite conversation of the scarlet damsel whenever she visited his shop.

On one occasion, after she made her selection and paid for it, she said she understood that Mr. Timmons was originally from Britain. The jeweler replied that indeed he was. Miss Lorry then told him that she had some real English plum pudding, and would he care to come and take tea with her upon the morrow? Besides, she had a large clock that needed repair and he could pick it up at the same time. He accepted the invitation. After all, drinking tea and eating real plum pudding—which he had not had in ever so long—would not endanger his immortal soul, would it?

The visit was pleasant, the tea itself was also English, and the plum pudding was excellent. They parted politely and he took the broken clock along with him. Jonathan Timmons had enjoyed his visit on the edge of sin and his conscience was clear, but this was not a story he cared to spread around. So he confided only in his brother, Thomas.

Jonathan's story about his adventure in the notorious North End fascinated Thomas because he liked English plum pudding, too. Thomas asked if he could return the repaired clock to Pearl Lorry's house—before the plum pudding ran out.

In a couple of days the clock was ready to be returned to its owner. Jonathan instructed his brother to be certain to place the clock on Pearl's mantel carefully because it had to be absolutely level to keep running. Then Jonathan wished him good luck with the plum pudding and sent Thomas on his way.

Thomas approached Pearl Lorry's house and knocked on the door, the expensive clock tucked securely under his arm, and his mouth set for delicious plum pudding. The door opened and standing before him was one of Pearl's ladies—naked as the day she was born.

Poor shy Thomas! He took one quick, horrified look and was so shocked that he forgot all about plum pudding and making sure the clock was set on a level surface. He dropped it on a nearby chair and ran as fast as he could back to the respectable part of town where ladies did not answer the door

According to information on the back of the
photograph, this young lady, whose name was Rose,
earned her living as a sporting girl in Aberdeen,
Washington.

unless they had all their clothes on.

But life for the sporting girls in the Northwest was not all
champagne and plum pudding; it was often a running battle
with the forces of good and sometimes with each other. There
was one incident in Baker, Oregon (then known as Baker City),
where two rival girls of the line holed up in their neighboring
cabins exchanging gunfire for half an hour. No one was
injured, but business no doubt dropped right off that day.

Hot, undisciplined tempers were common among many of the
brothel girls, and there were numerous accounts of quarrels
being settled with knives and guns, as well as with fist and
claw. Fights between the bawdy belles were so common on the
board sidewalks of Aberdeen's Paradise Alley and Heron
Streets that on a good night droves of drinking sailors and
loggers would take their beers and whiskies outside to watch
the action.

Sporting girls wait for some action in this 1897 view of the Eagle Saloon in Aberdeen, Washington.

Another pose by the girls of the Eagle Saloon. These ladies provided comfort to seamen and loggers in rooms over the saloon.

And the girls were never popular with the reformers, of course, who would decide from time to time to clean up a town. There was an episode recorded in Ellensburg, Washington, where a civic improvement group had a red-light house dragged away by a team of eight huge horses, with the stubborn doves still inside.

The shady ladies could be quite obstreperous on occasion, as in an incident reported in the Jacksonville, Oregon, *Democratic Times.* A fallen angel was arrested on a day in 1884 for using "profane and indecent language." She had a hearing that afternoon before Justice Huffer. The said angel "vehemently denied the charge in terms so strong that His Honor turned pale and nearly fainted."

Some of the doves were unpopular for various reasons. A nymph known as Irish Kate fell into disfavor in 1889. She burned down the entire city of Spokane!

Across from the old Northern Pacific Railroad depot, a couple of one-and-a-half-story wooden buildings had been taken over by Sam Wolfe—one for a saloon and the other for a restaurant called Wolfe's Lunch Counter.

Irish Kate lived and worked out of the rooms over the saloon. It seems that one day she had been drinking and went up to her rooms to fix her hair. It was Sunday, August 4, 1889. She was heating her curling iron in the glass chimney of a kerosene lamp, when in wandered a drunk wanting to purchase her services. He was a bit pushy and when she said no, they began to scuffle. In the ensuing wrestle the lamp was knocked over and started a fire. An open window provided a good draft and some lace curtains sped the great fire on its way.

Kate had time only to grab a few belongings and dash out. All the buildings in town were tinder dry from the August heat and the fire spread quickly. Before it was extinguished almost all of the downtown area of Spokane lay in smoldering ruin.

Other fires in other towns were said to have been caused by negligent "ladies upstairs." Though in some instances the girls may have been blamed unjustly, there is no doubt that a great many of them acted in ways flighty and irresponsible. But then, they were not paid to be responsible.

CHAPTER FOUR

Pleasure Palaces
of Portland

No one can say just who was the first member of the sisterhood to set up shop along the shores of the Willamette River, but she more than likely crossed the plains in one of the earliest covered wagons.

It was not until Miss Nancy Boggs arrived in Portland, however, that the profession began to show some sign of organization and efficiency. Where Nancy came from is clouded in the imperfect records of the time, and where she went is just as mysterious. But it is a fact that she opened an establishment in Portland in 1870 and was destined to do business for more than two decades.

Nancy's place of business for ten of those years was an immense river scow, some eighty feet long by forty feet wide. It was painted a bright crimson and was anchored in the middle of the river. The lower part was a saloon and dance hall and on the upper two floors there were rooms for ten to fifteen girls. Guests reached Nancy's place by small boats provided by the house. Nancy's establishment gave new meaning to the word "houseboat."

Madam Boggs' barge was moved occasionally, according to the demands of commerce, just as sport fishermen now move from place to place on the river in an attempt to guess where the fish are biting.

The floating palace was for many years a happy arrangement in that Nancy paid no liquor fees to either Portland nor to the city of East Portland, on the east side of the river. Raids by the police of both cities were met by heavy streams of water from a pump on the scow.

There were recurring floods of the Willamette, each spring and fall, but Nancy was an excellent navigator. It is reported that during the high water of 1876, the highest until 1894, she and her girls manned the unwieldy ship in a masterful fashion.

But the police of the two shore cities finally became so harassing that Nancy sold her ark and opened a parlor house in North Portland, on Pine Street between Second and Third.

Nancy's Pine Street house was not the most genteel parlor house in the city, as we note in this *Daily Oregonian* item of February 19, 1880: "Lively Row—About half past nine o'clock last night the ladies and gentlemen who attend the soirees at Nancy Boggs' palace on Pine Street became out of humor over

This was the not-so-genteel parlor house of Portland's madam Nancy Boggs, located on Pine Street, between Second and Third. Photo circa 1888.

some slight incident and began to smash each other over the head with bottles, chairs, beer mugs, etc. Officer Bramman happened to drop in and escorted two of the gentlemen, Alex Kidd and John Fagan to the city jail."

Nancy operated in Portland until 1894, when she left for parts unknown.

A contemporary of Nancy's for awhile was the capable Bridget Gallagher. Bridget also ran a scow for a brief time, but customers were always falling overboard, which sobered them to the extent that they left immediately for home when rescued. So Bridget, too, went to dry land and continued to operate a parlor house for at least ten years. She then moved to San Francisco, happily married.

Portland quickly grew in importance as the major shipping and commercial center south of Seattle and in the 1880s and early '90s a large number of elegant parlor houses were established, along with countless brothels of lesser distinction, to accommodate the burgeoning customer rolls. The madams and girls were mostly left alone by the authorities as long as they paid their monthly fines and caused no trouble. But once in awhile an upper class house was shut down by a police chief anxious to please certain of the moral city leaders. That is what they tried to do to Della Burris in 1895.

Miss Della Burris, of 150 Park Street, operated one of the most elaborate parlor houses in town. Her place was no joint. It was patronized largely by men who made their mark in the city's professional and business life.

The specific charge brought against Della, in April 1895, was of operating a bawdy house. That was the exact term used for her genteel establishment—bawdy house.

Della took time off from her many duties and went to court for a day. She pleaded not guilty. How right she was in so doing may be judged by the findings of Justice Geisler, who ruled thusly in Della's case: "Common fame and general reputation are not sufficient evidence to convict anyone of keeping a bawdy house. The positive fact of lewdness must be established beyond all reasonable doubt. . . Case dismissed." It seems they could not find anyone to testify against her.

The demure Miss Burris smilingly thanked the judge, got into her smartly turned-out carriage waiting outside the courthouse, and returned to 150 Park Street. She had been gone all of an hour-and-a-quarter, but she was such a lover of the hearth that she told her girls she was awfully glad to be home again.

In the decade of the 1890s, Portland was known along the Pacific Coast as a wide open city. Not all of it was, of course, but the North End (roughly Burnside north to the river) and the many parlor houses scattered throughout the city gave Portland a deserved reputation for easily available sin. Near the turn of the century a vice commission report showed

Miss Della Burris operated this elaborate parlor
house on Portland's Park Street. Her clientele
included many of the city's business and
professional leaders.

The dark-eyed miss in this photo was a Portland red-light lady called
"Spanish Clara." The portrait style and her appearance indicate that she
was a parlor house girl of class. Photo circa 1885.

around four hundred brothels, of various classes, present in the Rose City.

Though most of the bawdy belles worked in the North End, the parlor house madams held forth mostly south of Burnside. Miss Dora Lynn operated what she was pleased to call "a refined resort" at 269 Salmon, near Fourth; Minnie Reynolds' place was at Fifth and Washington, next door to the Star Hotel; Dora Clark and Maud Morrison were at Sixth and Stark, and redheaded Flora Hoyt and her girls had quarters at 130 Fifth Street.

The celebrated Madam Lida Fanshaw, acknowledged queen of parlor house operators, had her Mansion of Sin in a huge, beautiful Victorian house at 151 Seventh Street (now Broadway). She was almost across the street from the city's largest and most honored hostelry, the Portland Hotel, right in the heart of the business district. Hers was the best of the Portland houses of ill repute, visited by many of the substantial professional and business leaders of the city. There was nothing more elegant or refined, according to reports of the day, even in the larger and more sinful San Francisco.

The one and only Madam Lida Fanshaw took extreme pride in her exalted position, and she looked and acted the part. The statuesque brunette was never seen in public or private without her finest jewels, furs, and gowns. She imported her dresses and hats from Paris and London long before the wealthy society ladies of Portland began doing so. She had two ornate carriages for her promenades around town; one was a gleaming white with black trim and red roses, the other was an enclosed glass-paned vehicle, done in shiny black and gold. The former was her summer buggy, the latter protected her from the chill and wet of Oregon winters.

Madam Fanshaw and her girls were extremely polite, but you did not sit around her place a great while without spending substantial sums of money. It was no place for the loggers, miners, and fishermen. The house at 151 Seventh Street was kept elegant and opulent only by the lavish spending of Portland's richer young bloods and their fathers. The list of callers at Madam Fanshaw's in the 1890s, according to old-timers, would have shocked their wives and pastors.

A long gone Portland newspaperman once recollected an

Liz Stratford, pictured above, also known as Liz York, was a favorite at
Lida Fanshaw's Mansion of Sin in Portland.

occasion when a prominent man of affairs and his son accidentally met in Lida Fanshaw's parlor; the son arriving, the father leaving. This was embarrassing, and it was also something that seldom happened in a place so expertly run as Madam Fanshaw's.

But the infamous North End was where the rollicking, spirited action was to be found. Also known as Whitechapel, the North End was home to open vice in all its basic forms. Here one could visit Liverpool Liz and her Senate Saloon and Rooms, or dainty Mary Clark and her sin house called Ivy Green, or Sallie Brown and her Bella Vista Lodging House.

Liverpool Liz, one of Portland's well-known sporting girls, was later the proprietress of the infamous Senate Saloon.

The occasion for this young lady's stern visage may be the fact that in 1912 she was one of the most arrested *filles de joie* in Portland's North End. She is Elsie Savan of the Auditorium Rooming House.

Miranda Hall, early 1900s Portland
"businesswoman," held forth at 310 Flanders Street.
She was a second cousin to Chief of Police Slover.

Sallie once hung a sign in her parlor which read:

"Union House
Price: $2.00"

Here, too, were the brothels of Emma Corks, Tillie Mitchell, Pearl St. Clair, Jennie Miller, and Nelly Bly (yes, really). The houses operated by these ladies and many others lined the streets in the North End; Couch, Davis, Everett, Flanders, Glisan, Hoyt, Irving Streets; North First, Second, Third Avenues—all the way out to around Twenty-third Avenue. The

North End was big, sinful, and profitable.

Madam Louise Gautier and her wild and infamous Richelieu Rooms at Sixth and Couch was a North End favorite. Louise, a large Rubens-type lady, used to say that Portland was the best town on the Coast for her kind of business.

The well-known Merchants Hotel, still standing at 200 N.W. Davis, was built in 1885 and served as a North End red-light house for over twenty years before it was used for other much more legitimate enterprises.

Madge "Big Maddy" Cahill, and her partner, Charles May, owned and ran a string of brothels and saloons on Flanders Street. Their base of operations was the Welcome Saloon, from which they kept an eye on their mini-vice monopoly.

Portland was also the home of a certain establishment known from Canada to Mexico as the Paris House. The Paris House was opened in 1904 by a group of prominent Portland businessmen, including a well-known banker and a former mayor, for the pleasure of interested males among the thousands of visitors expected for the Lewis and Clark Exposition of 1905. In reality, more than 2.5 million people visited the first large exposition of international character ever held in the far western latitudes during its 137-day run. The Paris House proved to be a gold mine.

The Paris House was a block-long, rambling building that ranged from Third to Fourth on Davis Street. It was Portland's first really large brothel. This monstrous pleasure palace opened with exactly one hundred available doves. There were also saloons and a restaurant in the building.

A Mr. Duke Evans was the first manager of the Paris House, but when the backers learned he was getting light-fingered with the profits he was fired forthwith. Jim Phillips was the next manager and he continued in that capacity until Mayor Harry Lane, in a 1907 politically motivated, well-publicized, gigantic anti-vice campaign, closed exactly one house of ill repute; the Paris House.

Portland's recognized red-light district, the North End, was finally closed in 1912, when Mayor A. G. Rushlight, under pressure from the "good" faction in town, conducted an investigation into the bordello business in the city. Many of the well-mannered, low profile parlor houses were in the city's

Portland madam Louise Gautier, of the Richelieu
Rooms at Sixth and Couch Streets, was known as
Goldie Gray in her earlier days on the Barbary Coast.

Madge Cahill ran her business from Portland's
Welcome Saloon.

Several working girls are visible in this turn of the century view of Couch Street brothels in Portland's North End.

"aristocratic section." While around the courthouse, the police station, and the river there was an average of three brothels to every block.

And somewhat disconcerting to a city of churches was the quaint fact that "a person might stand on the roof of one of the principal churches of the city and throw a stone into any one of fourteen immoral places."

The mayor's Vice Commission examined hundreds of land titles to discover the true property owners of the red-light houses. It had always been known that some of the wealthiest pioneer families of Portland, as well as all of the Northwest cities, achieved much of their early success and power by trading indirectly on the vice business. The Pacific Northwest had always been a robust, free and easy country where prostitution, gambling, and liquor were highly profitable enterprises. They were particularly so to members of the establishment who owned the property but who did not feel any personal responsibility for its use.

The Vice Commission found that the real owners of the

This unidentified miss was one of the North End girls.

By 1900 many of the older wooden houses of ill repute in Portland's North End were taking on a worn-out look.

Portland's famous Erickson's Saloon on Second at Burnside boasted the longest bar in the world. From the 1890s until the 1920s seamen, townsmen, and loggers visited sporting girls in the small closed cribs around the balcony (seen here at the right of the photograph).

bordellos and the ground they sat upon included lawyers, doctors, bankers, prominent businessmen, city officials, church corporations, and even members of the Vice Commission itself.

These revelations brought about an unusual and gossip-engendering city ordinance, called the "tin plate law," which required that the owners of buildings inscribe their name and address on a tin plate and affix it to their building. The ordinance was designed to shame the well-placed owners of brothels into evicting their tenants.

After a decent interval, up went the name plates, all around the city, and it became a game of passers-by to spot the names of well-known city fathers nailed to the walls of bordellos. Some well-bred squirming took place until an attorney noticed a loophole; the ordinance failed to require that the owner's name be in English. As a result, some plates went up in Chinese, Sanskrit, Arabic, and Hebrew.

The year 1912 is remembered as the end of the open tenderloin and parlor houses in Portland. It also marked the close of much of the Rose City's colorful past.

CHAPTER FIVE
Sin on the Sound

The origin of the sporting house business in Seattle is closely linked with the name of John W. Pennell. In 1861 John built the first pleasure palace in the boisterous, lusty, woman-starved mill town. Prior to his arrival, the loggers and workers at Henry Yesler's mill were hard put to find any available ladies to be sinful with. There were only about two hundred people in town and fewer than one in ten were female. It was rare to find a girl over the age of fifteen who was not spoken for. And there were no bawdy belles available at all.

Enter John Pennell.

John hailed from San Francisco's Barbary Coast where he had been the successful proprietor of several brothels. It is not known for certain why he left to follow his fortune north, but it probably had something to do with the pressing competition of the hundreds of similar establishments in that fair city. The new town called Seattle, up in the Washington Territory, he heard, did not even have *one*.

Soon after his arrival, John built a large rectangular building of rough boards, housing a dance floor, a long bar, and a number of small private rooms where the primary business would be conducted. This structure, Seattle's first bordello, was located on fill land south of where the logging skid road came down to Henry Yesler's mill (now Yesler Way). Pennell's property and the adjacent area had been formed mostly of sawdust deposited from the mill. A man visiting John's establishment was said to be going "Down on the Sawdust," a term that endured for some time after other like business came into the area.

John Pennell called his place the Illahee, a Chinook Jargon

This 1868 photograph shows downtown Seattle in John Pennell's day. The
view is of Mill Street, the old logging skid road down to Henry Yesler's
mill. It is now called Yesler Way. The red-light district developed south of
Yesler (to the right of the photo).

This is a photo of Seattle from Beacon Hill, circa 1880. The Lava Bed
red-light district is to the top right of the tracks. The district expanded
when the area to the right of the curve was filled. Today the Kingdome
occupies the site.

word meaning "home place." And since there were no white women of the soiled dove persuasion in Seattle at the time, John staffed the Illahee with dusky Indian ladies, properly dressed and perfumed. His business became quite popular among loggers and seamen in the woman-sparse Puget Sound country and John prospered quickly.

Several years later John Pennell decided it was time for Phase Two of his plan. He returned briefly to San Francisco where he recruited a dozen or so *filles de joie* with promises of a golden future. And soon, debarking gaily from a ship tied up at the Seattle dock, came a dainty parade of silk stockinged loveliness—perfumed, rouge-cheeked, chattering white nymphs of the night—ready to greet the boys. They were the first white women north of the Columbia River to practice the world's oldest profession. Guided by their industrious boss, the merry group headed straight for the Illahee. And John Pennell was really in business.

Soon other entrepreneurs followed John's lead and the sawdust fill began to sprout additional pleasure palaces. The area south of the skid road, down on the sawdust, became Seattle's famous, notorious, and permanent red-light district. In years to come it would rival San Francisco's Barbary Coast.

About the time John Pennell was hitting his stride in the late 1860s, another forward-thinker emerged in the form of one Benjamin Sprague. He was actually Captain Benjamin Sprague, of the steamboat *Gin Palace Polly*. His idea was to divert some of John Pennell's customers before they reached the Illahee. The way he figured to do that was by bringing sporting girls and whiskey to the boys right at their logging camps around the Sound—save them the long trip to Seattle, you see.

Steaming around to the camps, and spending one day and night at each, made Captain Ben and his merry crew very popular with the woods boys longing for female companionship.

Unfortunately, Sprague and the *Gin Palace Polly* were in business only a short while before Ben had to take a forced two year vacation in jail—some misunderstanding with the authorities over selling liquor to Indians.

Seattle's population rose from around two hundred at the time of John Pennell's arrival to 3,550 in 1880, and it continued

This sloe-eyed miss was one of Seattle's Lava Bed girls.

Tacoma, 1871. John Pennell, Seattle's early vice king, opened a branch
sporting house here—Tacoma's first—in 1873.

to increase by 3,500 each year for the next decade. Great
lumber operations were established in the area, the shipping
business was booming, and rich coal deposits had been
discovered nearby. The economy was solid and Seattle was
bustling, and so was life south of Yesler in the district that
came to be called the "Lava Bed."

In the early 1880s, madams and girls from all over began
drifting to Seattle where the future seemed profitable. Most of
the "laundresses" and "seamstresses" established themselves
in the Lava Bed, where for blocks there stretched unbroken
lines of saloons, boxhouse theaters, gambling joints, and
countless brothels of varying sizes, classes and specialties.
Some of the madams and doves whose names are still recorded
were Jenny Sills, Lil DuPree, Laura Molloy, Mattie Singleton,
and Goldie McClure.

Among all of them grew up a certain feeling of kinship; they
were the Tenderloin, and the world north of Yesler led a
separate life unrelated to theirs. "Anything you like, Mister,
any way you like it."

Meanwhile, the high-class parlor house madams were moving
into Seattle, too, and right into mansions north of Yesler. The
decade of the 1880s saw the arrival of such luminaries in the
pleasure business as Lila Young, Rae McRoberts, Belle
Bernard, Clara Dumont, and the undisputed queen of them all,

Madam Lou Graham.

As in all of the booming new cities of the Northwest, Seattle's Better Element made periodic attempts to clean up the red-light district. But the law enforcers looked the other way and grand juries generally refused to indict the operators of bawdy houses. After all, the Lava Bed ladies were keeping pretty much to their district, and the sedate uptown parlor houses caused no trouble. And besides, everyone was paying her fair share in monthly fines, the total yearly tallies of which added very significantly to the coffers of the city treasury. Indeed, at one point it was determined that all the fines and license fees generated from the ladies of sin and their cohorts in the liquor and gambling trades amounted to fully eighty-percent of the entire General Fund.

The pleasure business was big business, and big business was welcome in Seattle.

Then there was a fire.

On June 6, 1889, a sleepy workman let a glue pot that had been heating on a stove boil over, starting a small fire. That

Laura Molloy, a south of Yesler "seamstress."

Jenny Sills, popular nymph of the night in Seattle, as
she appeared in the 1880s.

was at 2:40 in the afternoon. By about three the next morning, the entire business district and waterfront and Lava Bed had been burned to the ground; one hundred and twenty acres— sixty-six city blocks. The one blessing was that not a person was killed.

With all the downtown buildings completely engulfed, the fire had rapidly spread south into the congested red-light district with its labyrinth of bordellos, saloons, cafes, and dance halls. It had taken nearly thirty years to develop the Lava Bed from the early days of John Pennell's Illahee into a famous, world-class sin district. It took less than thirty minutes for it to be totally destroyed.

With the vigorous spirit that typified all of Seattle, the madams and girls of the Tenderloin set about to immediately rebuild what was lost. Those of the Better Element who thought the fire had wiped out the sporting district for good were disappointed to see new brick buildings, larger and gaudier than the old frame ones, going up on the same sites of the former establishments.

Until the new buildings were ready, many of the girls continued practicing their profession in tents set up alongside

"Anything you like, Mister, any way you like it."

Ida Bell, shown here, was a damsel of Seattle's
Tenderloin around 1900.

temporary canvas saloons, stores, and restaurants.

The area south of Yesler came back stronger and feistier after the Great Fire of 1889, but it was not the Lava Bed any longer; now it was Seattle's Tenderloin—and it was here to stay.

Seattle ushered in the next decade with optimism and high spirits. The population had jumped dramatically after the fire to 43,000. And no one in town was riding higher than the girls of the Tenderloin and the posh parlor houses scattered through the city. But by 1893 the entire country was in a great depression, including the Pacific Northwest. While much commerce in Seattle stagnated and slowed to a stop, life south of Yesler went on though not as gaily or profitably as in days past.

The year 1897 began on the same dismal note. The firmly

This Webster and Stevens photo captured the arrival of the steamer *Portland* with its "two tons of gold." The girls of Seattle's Tenderloin were ready.

Seattle became the primary outfitting and departure center for the Klondike. Multitudes of would-be millionaires had a last fling with Seattle's bawdy belles before heading north.

This is a photograph of Tillie Mitchell who was employed by Seattle madam Rae McRoberts to oversee a second parlor house in another part of the city.

This 1905 photograph shows part of Seattle's Tenderloin. Taken from Fifth and King Streets.

established parlor houses and Tenderloin bordellos were kept in business by customers hungry to buy fleeting comfort from their business troubles. Indeed some of the more prosperous madams depended in large part on a few wealthy clients for the continuance of their opulent life style—for in any economic reversal there are those who never seem to lose their financial footing. But the city business community in general, including the ladies in the pleasure business, were in trouble.

Then, suddenly, the trouble ended with the tumultuous cry guaranteed to gladden the heart of any working girl: "*GOLD!*"

On the morning of July 17, 1897, the steamer *Portland*, fresh from the Yukon River, docked in Seattle with the first dose of medicine to cure any depression: a cargo containing over two tons of Klondike gold.

Two days before, another steamer, the *Excelsior*, had put into San Francisco with nearly a half-ton of gold, and the wires carried word north that a second and richer shipment was enroute to Seattle. Thus, at six o'clock on the morning of July 17, about five thousand people were on hand at Schwabacher's Wharf to greet the gold ship. And the girls were fixing their hair.

The sixty-eight sourdoughs who debarked from the *Portland* that morning, straining under the weight of their duffel bags and suitcases, brought the beginning of golden days for Seattle and the sporting girls.

News of the great Klondike strike swept the country like wildfire and soon Seattle's streets were crowded with thousands of men headed to the gold fields; men ready for a last fling before shipping north. Nymphs of the night, too, flocked to Seattle. Most stayed to mine the miners, but some went north to Skagway and Dawson to be closer to the original source of their good fortune.

During the next few years multitudes of returning miners seemed so burdened with their heavy pokes and money belts that the ladies of pleasure felt it was their humanitarian duty to lighten the loads. That philosophy was officially backed by Mayor Tom Humes and the city council; the town ran wide open. The old Barbary Coast was definitely outclassed by this

Annie Redoubt helped to manage one of Mayor Hiram Gill's bordellos, the Midway. There were rooms for one hundred girls.

This 1910 photo is identified as Seattle dove "Jenny,
of the Midway," referring to a large Tenderloin
establishment linked to Mayor Hiram Gill.

time—Seattle was more wicked and wilder and running twenty-four hours a day. The red lights were burning brightly. Parlor house madams and the hundreds of girls south of Yesler rolled out the red carpets for the returning victors. And with new major strikes at Nome in 1899 and Fairbanks in 1902, the gold kept coming.

By 1900 Seattle's population had jumped to 81,000 and in 1910 it had exploded to 237,000. The year 1910 brought another explosion as well: Mayor Hiram C. Gill and his plans for the world's largest bordello.

Gill had been the leading lawyer for most of the parlor house madams and many of the Tenderloin girls. Ever the consummate politician, he worked himself onto the Seattle city council, then served as its president.

In 1910 Hi Gill ran for mayor on a "reform" platform that somehow included keeping the red-light district intact. Actually, his view was that by maintaining and controlling a Restricted District, and strictly enforcing prostitution laws elsewhere in the city, the ladies who were practicing their trade all over town—to the consternation of the Better Element—would move back south of Yesler. "Give 'em the Tenderloin and keep 'em out of the rest of the town."

It worked, he was elected.

One of the mayor's first acts was to install his old friend and business associate, Charles W. "Wappy" Wappenstein as chief of police. Wappenstein, and experienced and able grafter, was the perfect middleman to buffer Mayor Gill from pointed questions raised about his connections to the sin business. Wappy would control things directly, and the mayor would benefit as the idea man.

Within six months after his inauguration, Gill had his police chief put two of their Tenderloin associates, Clarence Gerald and Gideon Tupper, in charge of the two largest bordellos south of Yesler, the Midway and the Paris House (no relation

Seattle Mayor Hiram Gill's world's largest bordello. This building and an annex were planned for 500 sporting girls.

Two turn of the century Pacific Northwest sporting ladies.

to the one in Portland). The Midway had rooms for one hundred girls, the Paris could accommodate seventy. Business was good and everybody profited. The city was soon back to being run wide open.

Then Hiram Gill and Company got an idea that was grand, ambitious, and marvelous. The only problem was that it was so outrageous it also got Hi recalled right out of office.

Gill and his friends, Wappenstein, Gerald, and Tupper, not content with the proceeds already coming in from the Tenderloin, decided to build the biggest, grandest bordello the world had ever seen. It would have *five-hundred girls* and it would be right there in Seattle—a world attraction.

The location chosen for this grandiose enterprise was Beacon Hill, overlooking the Tenderloin. Tupper and Gerald were to be the front men. They formed the Hillside Improvement Company and had no trouble selling stock to finance the venture.

But there was one small problem: part of the proposed site for the massive five-hundred room structure was right in the

This 1911 photograph shows stairs leading to a brothel in Seattle's Tenderloin south of Yesler.

middle of Tenth Avenue South—a city street. However, to no one's real surprise, Hi Gill's obliging city council thoughtfully granted Hillside Improvement, whose initials, you may have notice, were HI, a fifteen-year lease to the street. The building was completed, but it was never used for its intended purpose.

The Better Element in town had seen enough of Hi Gill even before the completion of the Beacon Hill bordello—they wanted him out. A recall petition was filed and the election took place in February 1911. The pro-Gill forces included five-hundred nymphs from the Tenderloin, who marched to City Hall en masse to vote. But their support was not enough to save the good mayor and he was ousted from office.

And his world's largest bordello? It became an innocent apartment house and stood until 1951, when an errant Air Force bomber from Boeing Field crashed into it.

Seattle's sporting ladies retained a high-spirited self-reliance through ensuing cleanup efforts which eventually changed the face of the Tenderloin. For many years of the lively fun-loving city's history, the ladies of pleasure personified the robust, sportive soul that was at the heart of the Queen City. There never truly was a definitive velvet curtain drawn between uptown society and the ladies south of Yesler. There was seepage both ways. Husbands and sons from the hill would drift down to the parlor houses or the Lava Bed to visit the bawdy belles. And ā bright working girl with the right dash and endearing charms could—and did—marry a millionaire from the Better Element. The ladies of the red lights were a significant part of the life and story of Seattle.

CHAPTER SIX

The Jane Barnes Story

The first white woman ever to set foot in the Pacific Northwest surely deserves mention in a book on the naughty ladies of the Northwest because she was a courtesan. Her name was Jane Barnes and the story of this sportive miss is a delightful one. It all started with Donald McTavish and his penchant for blondes.

In 1818 a wealthy, middle-aged Scot named Donald McTavish was appointed governor of Fort George, the name the North West Fur Company had given to John Jacob Astor's trading post, Astoria, at the mouth of the Columbia River. Britain had captured the post and McTavish had come out of retirement to oversee the fort.

The new governor was temporarily in Portsmouth, England, outfitting his ship, the *Issac Todd*, with generous stores of necessary staples—fine wines, tinned roast beef, and rich cheeses. But he was missing a staple he very much desired. McTavish was, as an acquaintance put it, "of an amorous temperament." In particular, he liked lively blondes. And there were none of the "fair but frail" persuasion waiting for him on the Columbia River, because there were not any anywhere to be found on the Northwestern coast of America.

He was pondering his problem in the taproom of his hotel when he spied a well-rounded, pretty, young blue-eyed barmaid named Jane Barnes. And she was blonde. Being a plain-spoken man, Donald McTavish made the fair Jane a quasi-indecent business proposition. If she would accompany him to Fort George, he would provide her with a lavish wardrobe of dresses and hats and whatever other finery she should desire. And upon their return to England he would guarantee her a generous annuity for the rest of her life. Marriage was definitely not in the plan.

One of Jane's admirers said that she "consented to become *le campagnon du voyage* of Mr. McTavish in a temporary fit of erratic enthusiasm." But after all, the offer was a tempting one and Jane Barnes may have relished the thought of becoming the first white woman to set foot on the northwest coast of America. Not to speak of her excitement at trunks filled with fine dresses and other presents, and the prospect of a lifelong annuity upon her return to England.

McTavish and his pretty mistress were on the high seas for a year and a month before anchoring in the Columbia River off Fort George. As the *Issac Todd* lay anchored that morning of April 24, 1814, a small sloop from the fort came alongside. The little boat still bore the name *Dolly* in honor of John Jacob Astor's wife, as the British occupiers had not yet rechristened the captured craft.

Among those in the reception committee from Fort George was Alexander Henry, Jr., a very prim and proper young man, who wrote peevishly in his journal, "McTavish was just up. He met me on the deck, and we went into the cabin where I was introduced to Jane Barnes." Henry was astonished to discover a white woman—a courtesan—in the new governor's cabin.

The proud McTavish invited Alexander Henry and other Fort George officials to dine aboard the *Issac Todd* that evening, where they could cast approving eyes on the beauteous Jane. As expected, she delighted the entire complement at Fort George—all male. They agreed immediately that the sloop *Dolly* must be renamed *Jane* in honor of the governor's mistress.

Alexander Henry soon softened toward Jane Barnes, and indeed began feeling a close attachment to her. The record does not indicate that she rebuffed his attention. During one of Henry's visits to the *Todd*, he dined again with McTavish and Jane. She was still living aboard the ship as there were no spare quarters adequate for her in the crudely constructed fort. Henry later wrote tersely in his journal of that evening, "A vile discourse took place, in the hearing of Jane, on the subject of venereal disease and Chinook ladies."

A few days later, Henry offered Jane the use of his room at

the fort. She accepted, and he noted in his journal: "The longboat came with Jane, bag and baggage.... About sunset the jolly-boat took Mr. D. McTavish on board alone. Jane, of course, remained, having taken up her lodging in my room." Why Miss Barnes left the ship to stay at the fort is not clear. Perhaps she was tiring of McTavish, or he of her.

In days to come, Jane ruled the fort like a queen, flouncing about and flashing her saucy smiles and blonde curls at the rough fur traders and shy clerks. One day she would decorate her head with feathers and flowers, and the next she would braid her long golden tresses and wear no bonnet—always displaying her figure advantageously to the delight of the observers.

On May 17, the Jane-less McTavish consoled himself with the Chinook ex-wife of Astorian Benjamin Clapp. On that day Alexander Henry wrote in his journal disapprovingly that McTavish had clothed her "in fine black broadcloth which cost 23 shillings sterling a yard."

Five days later, Jane lost both her former and present protectors when McTavish and Henry were drowned while attempting to cross the Columbia. Though she was left suddenly alone, we can assume Jane found someone among the males at the fort eager to console her. The records do show that she turned down the fort's surgeon, Dr. Swann, when he offered a semi-permanent arrangement.

Some of the men at the post other than Alexander Henry kept journals, and history is indebted to Ross Cox for the following amusing scenario of Jane in action. It seems Jane, the unschooled barmaid from Portsmouth, had memorized a few literary quotations, probably during the long sea voyage, for use in conversation with the gentry at Fort George.

On a certain occasion, one of the Scottish clerks was chivalrously upholding the native women, whose character Jane was attacking. The Indians' unconcern over propriety in sexual conduct probably seemed to Jane an unflattering caricature of her own sexual indulgences. The clerk replied that their conduct was no worse than some white women he had known, and he glanced significantly at Jane.

"O, Mr. Mac!" Miss Barnes declared. "I suppose you agree with Shakespeare, that 'every woman is at heart a rake'?"

"Pope, ma'am, if you please," corrected the clerk, referring to the English poet.

"Pope! Pope!" replied Jane. "Bless me, sir, you must be wrong; 'rake' is certainly the word—I never heard of but one female Pope."

At the end of May, after four months at the fort, Jane boarded the *Issac Todd* and sailed for Canton, where she immediately captivated an English gentleman of great wealth connected to the East India Company.

She never did collect the lifelong annuity.

EPILOGUE
A Parting Glance

Those are some of the stories of the ladies who practiced the world's oldest profession in the raucous early days of the Pacific Northwest. There were countless others whose names are no longer recorded—many never were. Whether they plied their trade in a high-class city parlor house or a wild, rollicking variety theater or on the line at some out of the way gold camp, the madams and the girls of pleasure were a picturesque lot who could be found throughout Oregon and Washington.

At once maligned and applauded, banned and accepted, ignored and condoned, the women of the red lights were, as a group, big business and an interesting, colorful part of Pacific Northwest history. Ladies of easy virtue? Certainly. Sinners? Maybe. Not unlike people anywhere, some of the naughty ladies were good and some were not so good; many were thieves, many were honest; some were hopeful, others despaired; some were trustworthy, some were not worthy of trust.

Just like us.

Glossary

Every occupation has its own unique vocabulary, including the scarlet profession of the naughty ladies. This is a brief glossary of terms from the Northwest red-light trade in the nineteenth century. Though not a complete listing, these words and phrases were selected for their interest and origins.

Bagnio—(BAHN-YO) A house of prostitution. The word derived from the Italian *bagno*, or immoral public bathhouse. Bagnio was first used in the English language in the 1600s to mean a brothel.

Bawd—From the French word *baud*, or merry. It refers to a prostitute or other lewd lady.

Bawdyhouse—A brothel.

Boarding House—A term used by madams to describe their establishment. The girls were often referred to as "female boarders."

Bordello—A house of prostitution. The word is Italian for brothel, and is rooted in the old French word *bordel*, a cabin, hut, or brothel.

Boxhouse—A small theater ostensibly for variety stage acts, but in reality a brothel. The girls operated out of tiny second-and third-tier cubicles or "boxes."

Brothel—A house of prostitution. Its origin is in the old English word *brothern*, or ruined. The word once referred to the person and not the place. It was first recorded in print in 1493.

Courtesan—A prostitute or mistress. The term derived from the French, referring to a high-class royal court prostitute. It has been used in the English language since 1549.

Crib—A small dwelling for a prostitute. It originally meant a stall for an ox (in Middle English).

Cyprian—A prostitute. Named for the island Cypress, the home of Venus, mythical goddess of love. Cypress was noted for its temples of love, hence those who practiced Venus' art were called Cyprians.

Daughter of Joy—A prostitute.

Dove—A prostitute. A shortened version of "soiled dove."

Fair But Frail—A nineteenth century term for the sisterhood of prostitutes.

Fairy Belle—A prostitute. The source of the term was the sexual promiscuity of the legendary fairies.

Fille de Joie—A French term, meaning girl of joy, or prostitute.

Girl of the Line—A prostitute working out of a cabin in a small town (see "line").

Harlot—A prostitute. In Old English, the word referred only to an unchaste man.

Hooker—A purely American term referring to a prostitute. It originated during the Civil War when General Joseph Hooker allowed camp followers to operate near his Union troop posts.

Ladies of Joy—Prostitutes.

Lava Bed—One of the terms referring to Seattle's old red-light district south of Yesler Way.

Line—A common term for the prostitution district in small mining and logging towns. The line usually consisted of a row(s) of small houses or cabins along a narrow street at the edge of town.

Lower Town—The name given to Olympia's prostitution district.

Madam—The lady acting as "key executive" in a house of prostitution. The madam was the boss, bookkeeper, chief hostess, and "mother" to her girls. A good madam ran a well-ordered house and knew many secrets.

North End—A common term for Portland's prostitution district north and a little south of Burnside.

Nymph—A young lady of ultimate accessibility. A prostitute. Also known as "nymph of the night." The source of the term was the semi-divine beautiful young maidens of mythology, especially Greek, who inhabited woods, fountains, rivers, and lakes.

Painted Lady—A prostitute. It originates from the sometimes excessive amount of makeup used.

Parlor House—A high-class, often elegant, house of prostitution.

Pretty Waiter Girl—Prostitutes who worked in a boxhouse serving drinks and other delights. Some were pretty, some were not.

Red-Light District—The prostitution district of a town or city. The term originates from the habit of railroaders in Dodge City, Kansas, of hanging a red lantern on the door of an occupied prostitute.

Resort—In former times, a house of prostitution.

Restricted District—A prostitution district. In many Northwest towns and cities, prostitution was tolerated and kept within a certain area or neighborhood.

Shady Lady—A prostitute.

Soiled Dove—A prostitute. The term is often shortened to dove.

Soiree—(SWA-RAY) A French term meaning "evening party." It was first used in English printing in 1820.

Sporting Girl—A prostitute.

Sporting House—A house of prostitution. The term originally referred to an inn where sporting men gathered.

Strumpet—A prostitute. The origin of the word is obscure. It first appeared in English writing in the early 1300s.

Tenderloin—The red-light district. Originally, the area in New York City were there was the greatest concentration of brothels, gambling dens, saloons, and low theaters. It was a favorite assignment of police seeking graft.

Whitechapel—A common term for the red-light district of Portland, named for London's famous sin area.

Source Notes

There have been no prior books devoted solely to the red-light business of the old Pacific Northwest. Material found to be of use in the research for this book came from a wide variety of sources. Among these were letters, journals, diaries, reports, and notes located in the collections of the Washington State Historical Society (Tacoma, WA); the Oregon Historical Society (Portland, OR); the University of Oregon Library, General and Special Collections (Eugene, OR); the University of Washington Library, General and Special Collections (Seattle, WA); and various local historical societies, libraries, and individuals.

In addition, works published by noted Northwest history writers Murray Morgan, Gordon Newell, William Speidel, among others, were found to be helpful with information on the "girls" in western Washington. Murray Morgan's famous *Skid Road* contains valuable and fascinating studies of such Puget Sound characters as John Considine, Mayor Hiram Gill, and John Pennell, who started it all in Seattle. Also, Mr. Morgan's *One Man's Gold Rush* explains and shows in rare photographs what the Klondike madness was all about.

Bill Speidel's *Sons of the Profits* is an exhilarating look at the growth of Seattle—including some of her sins and secrets.

Gordon Newell's *Totem Tales of Old Seattle* has excellent stories about the Queen City, and his *Rogues, Buffoons, and Statesmen* is both a knowledgeable and hilarious examination of Olympia.

County records and old police files provided some specific data on various madams and girls.

The major source of material for this book was the old

newspapers of Oregon and Washington, from the mid-1800s through 1915. From the Seattle *Post Intelligencer* to the Portland *Oregonian* to the Baker City *Bedrock Democrat*, virtually all of the papers in the Pacific Northwest carried interesting accounts of the naughty ladies. The authors spent many hours examining microfilmed newspapers at the libraries of the University of Oregon and the University of Washington, both of which maintain excellent collections.

The photographs in this book came primarily from the Carl W. Davis collection, and many were used through the courtesy of various individuals and local historical societies in Oregon and Washington.

Carl W. Davis was an early twentieth century private researcher and collector of historical photographs dealing with bawdy belles of Washington, Oregon, and Los Angeles. Although he lived most of his later life in Southern California, his first love was the Pacific Northwest.

Mr. Davis' research led him to many sources now unavailable. He knew a number of the early century madams personally, and also police officials, journalists, and historians. From all of these, as well as from private collectors and photographers, he obtained a wealth of fine photographs of the Northwest's ladies of joy.

Carl W. Davis passed away in 1952 and many of his photos were acquired by the authors.

Index

Gething, Louise 22
Gill, Hiram 11, 63, 118, 119, 120, 121, 122
Gimletville 24
Gin Palace Polly 108
Golden Rule 15
Goldie Gray 101
Graham, Lou 1, 3, 7, 31, 40, 56, 57, 58, 59, 60, 61, 62, 63, 78, 111
Granite 16
Graves, Frank 47, 48
Graves, Mae 13
Grays Harbor 11

—H—

Hall, Miranda 99
Harbor, Julie 27, 28
Harner, Sadie 40
Heath, Mabel 40, 43
Henry, Alexander Jr. 125, 126
Heron Streets 87
Hillside Improvement Company 121, 122
Holmes, Minnie 36
Hoyt, Flora 95
Huffer, Justice 89
Humes, Tom 118
Huron Street 4
Hyde, Sam 47

—I—

Illahee 106, 108, 113
Irish Kate 89
Irish Moll 15, 72
Issac Todd 124, 125, 127
Ivy Green 97

—J—

Jacksonville 5, 48, 78, 89
James, Ada 72
James, Mollie 48, 49
Jane 125
Jerman, Edity 78
Johnson, Eve 34, 35, 36

—K—

Kahn, Bertha 36
Kidd, Alex 92
Kingdome 107
Klondike 14, 67, 115, 118
Klondike Kate 18, 19, 20, 22
Kneeland Hotel 78
Knight, Sophie 70
Koning, Mary 78
Kressler, Raymond T. 48

—L—

La Grande 27, 28
Lady X 69
Lane, Emma 80
Lane, Harry 100
Lava Bed 4, 107, 109, 110, 111, 113
Levi, Celia 55
Lewis and Clark Exposition 100
Light Handle Liz 24
Lion 14
Liverpool Liz 97
Loomis 67
Lorry, Pearl 84
Lower Town 4
Lucy Give 'Em Back 24
Lynn, Dora 95

—M—

Mack, Lillie 77
Mansion of Sin 3, 79, 95, 96
Marshfield 31, 32, 53, 54, 55
Matson, Johnny 22
May, Charles 100
McClure, Goldie 110
McGowan, Bill 23
McRoberts, Rae 6, 30, 40, 82, 83, 84, 110, 116
McTavish, Donald 124, 125, 126
Merchants Hotel 100
Merry Widow 14

Midway 118, 119, 120, 121
Miller, Jennie 99
Missoula 62
Mitchell, Tillie 99, 116
Molloy, Laura 110, 111
Monroe, Ella 64, 67
Morgan, Harry 21, 23, 77
Morrison, Maud 85, 95
My House Saloons 14

—N—

Nighthawk 70, 72
North End 3, 79, 84, 93, 95, 97, 98, 99, 100, 102, 103, 104
North West Fur Company 124

—O—

Oak Hotel 11
Ohben, Dorothea Georgine Emile 56
Olympia 4, 23, 35, 36, 78
Olympus 23
Opera Alley 4, 40
Oregon Hotel 11
Oregon Mare, The 24
Oregon Rose 1
Our Lady of Good Help Catholic Church 60, 63

—P—

Pacific Pride 56
Pantages, Alexander 20
Paradise Alley 87
Paris 121
Paris House 100, 120
Pendleton 11
Pennell, John 106, 107, 108, 110, 113
People's Theater 17, 18, 20
Phillips, Jim 100
Phillips, Kitty 20
Pioneer Saloon and Rooms 14